RECESS TIME

WHEN MIND GETS TO PLAY WITH MEMORY AND IMAGINATION

NICK WEBER

outskirts
press

Illuminating and intimate, Nick Weber's latest book, a collection of essays, Recess Time: When Mind Gets to play with Memory and Imagination, takes us on an extraordinary journey through and with what makes us human, what makes us alive. Channeling the spirit of Montaigne or E.B. White, and ranging through topics such as God, Earth, Humor, Sex, Food, and Infinity, Nick Weber's writing is playful, serious, philosophical, and hilarious. It's like a pub or café conversation you never want to leave, where Einstein, Shakespeare, God, and perhaps a four-year-old gorilla from the Milwaukee zoo just might stop by your table.

Kevin Curdt, Courtroom Clerk, Santa Clara County Superior Court, San Jose, CA

There is an entirety to these essays that play upon one another, from Measurement to Food, from Infinity to Animals. All are parts of the whole. And including Einstein and de Chardin and Shakespeare during Recess invites the reader to see the utter fun that they are, the way they call us not to the drudgery of learning, but to having a good time on the playground.

Judie Gillespie, Chair of Theology Department, Divine Savior Holy Angels High School, Milwaukee, WI

Recess Time, When Mind Gets to Play with Memory and Imagination, is a primer for any person serious about *becoming*. It doesn't just touch on all the topics of life: it meets them head on, toys with them from the edges of thought, and then neatly concretizes the Infinite, the Known Unknown, the Divine and the Unforeseen in a cozy blanket of fun and play. It will fuel many a conversation with the imagery, knowledge, humor, wit and downright laughter that only a master storyteller and philosopher like Nick Weber can offer.

Carlo Pellegrini, Co-founder of
Amazing Grace Circus, Circus Producer,
Director, Choreographer, Nyack, NY

Dedication
In memory of my late best friend, Mitch Kincannon,
who put up with my daydreams, allowing them
to bring joy to our audiences, and in gratitude
for Mitchell's current channel in my life, Kylle
St. Trail, who listens, challenges, and helps me
turn daydreams into helpful insights for life.

To John —
Finally a book about
your favorite class. You
were good at recess, much
better than the classroom.
Your buddy,
Oz

Table of Contents

INTRODUCTION

IT'S 5:15 A.M. I'm sitting in our front room by my-self. Very dark outside. Cold. I am absolutely free to write on this otherwise blank screen whatever I want. I have published two books, and this may also find its way to a public printing press.

Yet, even as a possible book looms, my early-morning keyboard twitches have little to do with freedom of the press. I am not free; I am compelled. If my twitches are sound, you are compelled. Otherwise, you wouldn't be into a second paragraph already.

But the reasons for my compulsion may be far from anything to do with the persuasive word flow that compels you. You see, I have to write. Everyone tells me that. Even my therapist. I am creative by nature, and I have lacked a form of creative expression for years.

As a result, I have been sick for years. Depressed to the extent that I can't get anything done. Nothing. But folks who know my abilities for self-expression have joined a chorus whose signature refrain is "Well, are you writing?"

Well, I am writing. And even as I press you into tracking me through these characters on a page or screen, I find a measure of freedom. Oh my. Is that freedom of the press?

But writing is just form. What is there of substance to be written about?

I would posit that the richest experience anyone has or can have is to be found when the mind wanders through the recesses of one's memory and imagination. These are the mind's recess times, not the overtly productive and organized efforts to figure something out, make a plan, or deliberately create. Gigantic surprises awake my daydreams, especially when I'm out for a walk and my mind senses that it, too, can be out to play. Recess time. Huge conceptual puzzles meet pants-down clown; insect-size images sting their way into my attention span as if they crawled out of the Grove of Academe. Selfishness meets Socrates. Sublimity plays with ridicule, and the minuscule triggers expanse. The trick is to recognize such moments as rich in relevance to ordinary, more structured life and thought. Stringing together subjects and predicates on a blank screen is the process serving such recognition. It's class time. In from recess, we revisit the mind's play and revel in the substance that becomes written expression.

Out for a walk, images prevail; judgments, with their firmer business of relating images to life or each other, have been left behind. Here at the computer, there is no key struck without constant judgment and evaluation. Here there isn't as much fun as recess, but there is the rich fulfillment of conception and even pregnancy.

So, what are typical recess-time playmates for me? Let's make them the chapters of this book. In fact they can be the titles of some consecutive essays: God, Integrity, Sex, You, Earth, Humor, Infinity, Measurement, Art, Food, Animals. That's enough. You don't have to be skipping down the Agora with Aristotle to notice that all those subjects relate to each other. And you don't have to be drunk with Shakespeare's Sir Toby Belch to see that "It's all one." That's the unity that gives the book a reason for covers.

But what gives me the right to saddle readers with my take on all this stuff? Where's my authority and experience in such matters?

Well, I do take walks, and I do daydream, indulge in recess time, rolling around in those recesses of a fairly rich imagination and a full memory. I have been on five continents; played fourteen of Shakespeare's characters professionally, touched the Taj Mahal and the Pyramid of Cheops, watched cremations from a boat on the Ganges, ridden a camel or two on the Sahara and an elephant in the American Circus, watched Blackfeet Indian kids play "cowboys and Indians," stood in Mohandas Gandhi's final bedroom, confronted two lone elephants on the African savannah, slept on the Yangtze, played hide and seek on the edge of the Amazon, wept in the Accademia of Firenze, taught literature and theater arts for over ten years, practiced as an ordained Jesuit priest who performed in his order's professional circus ministry for twenty-three years and picked up a couple of graduate drama and theology degrees, spent five years as a professional clown in large American circuses, wrote and performed nationwide in three one-man shows: "Shakespeare, Just for Fun!" "An Evening with Gerard Manley Hopkins," and "And Jesus Laughed!" I've proudly watched three former circus students perform professionally, taught retirees the works of Shakespeare for over ten years, walked and wept on the Agora of Athens, laughed at the Roman Forum, and marveled at a rainbow while descending into Machu Picchu.

A collection of essays such as this invites the spirit of discovery, the possibility of new connections between old ideas. An *essay* is, after all, a trial or test. Might there be relationships where we never suspected them?

More humbly, could it be that we have forgotten some connections we once took for granted?

In the recesses of the imagination and memory are eager subjects for the interplay that is creativity. In this collection, those subjects are freed for an interplay that yields alternative notions, concepts, and beliefs. And because the spirit of this collection is that of play, a comfort level with flippancy and punditry might be desirable. Little might be sacred, and the sacred found where it would be least expected. Play being the ritual of make-believe, surprise must be welcomed, not feared. And extended play, with and through surprises, could be supremely valuable. Hence, these playful essays.

The essays are connected, not the way plot developments in a novel are connected, but through the author's experiences of playful thought. Themes find their ways into subsequent contexts, and there are occasions when recess time may feel like romping through a hall of mirrors. And while the joyful spirit of play might predominate, the whole enterprise is undertaken in the hopes of discovering the serious holiness of new connections. That is, play cannot rule out serious and disciplined thought. Such thought is not to be feared but wondered at and then seen as a cause for laughter because we never noticed it before.

Finding a voice in the writing of these essays has

been quite a struggle. *I*, *you*, and *they* wiggle their ways into the text almost interchangeably. This has been troublesome, thought of as a weakness in style and undesirable. A walk past a schoolyard changed all that: it was recess time. Myriad voices interchanged and loving and not-so-loving addresses of *I*, *you*, *he*, and *she*, noisily blended into what every recess must be. Call it the cacophony of the casual or the charm of chant; it was a weave of energies bent on haphazard discovery *everywhere* with *everyone*.

Hopefully, there will be disagreement with some of the discoveries in this collection of attempts to uncover new relationships. Such opposition itself will posit new reflections and possibly new and more valuable connections. Long before Hegel's *concrete, abstract, absolute* became the *thesis, antithesis, synthesis* triad, humans encountered in the magnificent art of conversation the possibility of agreement *because of* differences. Because of the subject matter in certain passages, sentences find themselves in the conditional mood. Hence, there are plenty of *perhapses, it could/might bes,* and *maybes* throughout the essays.

In the best dream possible, the book could be seen as a modest work of art and the attributes discussed in the essay "Art" realized throughout the chapters. Then, perhaps, relationships between the essays become more evident. The emergence of such connections could be as enjoyable as a comfortable work of art. In that mode, relaxation, acceptance, and surprise might expand ordinary breathing to lightsome aspiration, the best preparation for the more structurally demanding tasks of life. After all, that bell ringing? It isn't calling us to math class. Let's play.

Author wondering where he left the Sphinx

GOD

POOR GUY. IMAGINE going through all eternity with a first name like that. At least the last name—damnit—lends the expression some rhythm, especially in the heat of frustration, say, the dropping of a fine glass of merlot, "Goddamnit." But *God?* Nor is the polite and non-committal substitute "Gosh" much of an improvement. At least *God* refers to something. Or does it?

Goddamnit, this is tough stuff. After millennia of *Zeus, Yahweh, Elohim,* and *Allah,* the root of all those millennia becomes *God.* And too many of the advocates of such a non-name have long ago become literal soldiers ripping other advocates apart for whatever the hell they think *God* means. So, forget anything like sound anthropology—even etymology—as deep grounding for theology. Cosmology? Took off with the last galaxy heading nowhere known. Yet.

And still so many believe, and what they believe they believe is as real as the next need to be prayed for. They believe in prayer, appeasing ritual (including the sacrifice of offspring, such as Isaac and Jesus), and eternal life replete with a gated community and (if you want them) harp lessons. All as real as the comfortable life they long to live. Given the innate and genuine goodness of so many, such criticism seems harsh, cruel, even false. But it is the respect for such goodness in neighbors that urges not only criticism and caution but outright rejection. A person's goodness alone is testimony of the soundness of their longing for the better, the greater, the more without naming it in accordance with traditional unprovable forces.

That longing. It's the universal and continuous force. We hanker, want, reach, and stretch, constantly pursuing some kind of *more.* Are we finished? Is there more work to be done on what we are? If a bird's beak in the Galapagos can enlighten us about ongoing development, shouldn't the discoveries in brain science, neurology, and human emotions suggest that maybe, just maybe, we aren't all here? Yet. And couldn't that very longing, that pursuit of more perfect states of being, be what we have named *God?* Could *Yahweh, Elohim,* and *Deus,* not to mention *Zeus, Athena, Brahma, Bhagwat,*

Vishnu, and *Guanyin*, also be worshipped as *Yetness* or *Need*? For all the so-called revelation throughout the history of religions, the names for the deity seem very limited in their own transparency about what those deities have achieved. Recently a student of mine from long ago invited me to his home to have dinner with him and his wife. After we sat down for the meal, we took hands, and my student led a prayer. "Let us thankfully pray to whatever deity Nick hasn't pissed off tonight!" Of course, laughter finished the prayer, but he has long known of my slim orthodoxy.

Perhaps we have been looking in the wrong places for the holy of holies. Perhaps our looking is what counts. What makes us "look"? What is the pure desire to know? There will be no argument that the seeking, longing, pursuit, or "looking" is forceful, filled with force. And if F=MA, mass times acceleration, we, above all, will want to investigate the basis for the acceleration. It is vital, strong, and universal.

So it is that a theological pursuit becomes a cosmological or downright physical pursuit. Enter Albert. Could it be that Einstein's search for a "unified field theory" explaining and unifying the forces of gravity and electromagnetism, itself evidence of an embracing need, is a theological, even a religious, quest? Inside of Einstein's own personal spirit, there is an energetic quest for a wholeness, an integrity of forces he perceives as so fundamental. It is this wholeness that propels and draws him through all his admitted mistakes and theoretical wrong turns (sins?) and back to his basic quest: Oneness. Like all of us, he dies reaching.

"Do you believe in God?"

"Uh, no." The "uh" is verbal cover for a mental reservation falling into place. "I do not believe in the God you most likely mean."

"Do you believe in God?"

"Uh, yes." Mental reservation again. "Yet it's a god that is not parental, but rather comprehensive of all desires, pursuits, imaginations, and active gains resulting from the force of yearning. The very energies that lead you to ask the question and my struggles to reply accurately are God." A mouthful and a mindful. But a heartful, too (with apologies to the neurologists who know where our emotions really come from). This very writing and the struggle for word-choice alignment with concept? God. Hey, in the old church replete with Irish missionaries that baptized and taught in Northern California, this might even be a sacrament. That's if some measure of grace (goodness) is gained in the reading. But wait: it isn't "instituted by Christ," as the catechism stipulates it should be.

Oh my. Another turn in the energy flow, and things are getting greasy. *Christ*, from the Greek *christos*, implies *chrism,* that waxy oil they put on you at baptism, confirmation, and the anointing of the sick. *Christ* is no more the last name of Jesus than *damnit* is the last name of God. It is only a footnote to let us know that Saint Paul and his companion believers were doing their homework. These folks were from the Jewish tradition and knew the prophecies about the messiah, the *anointed one* (that waxy oil again) who was to come and make things better and easier. All signs pointed to a wonderful, loving, and brave Galilean from Bethlehem. Just to know him was to feel enlarged, whole. But he was also an expert at identifying false gods because he had himself together unlike anyone his disciples had ever met. So, about twenty years after—and because of—the mess with the Roman city hall in occupied Jerusalem and after the gore of a nailed death on a wooden cross, the humble Jesus became *the Christ* everyone around him was waiting for.

"Do you believe Jesus was divine?"

"No more than you and I are divine. He was just gifted to know what *divine* meant and that he was part of that meaning."

I felt very strong in that reply because I have, for years, meditated on the universal participation in all things divine. I even felt that our conversation was divine. And I was fearless in front of my dear hostess, who was holding a handful of table knives when she asked the question. But what does *divine* mean? Is *divinity* real? That longing to be more, that reaching for wholeness is divine, and it is as real as our experience of it. Even Jesus was reaching.

Again, in that it matters at all, is this writing a sacrament? Will the old *Baltimore Catechism* recognize it as "instituted by Christ"?

Well, of course it's instituted by Christ. All the institutional messes over who and what he is and means? Instituted by Christ. Theologically I am a messy thinker because of the Christ issue in history. And I'm writing to clear up a little of the mess. For myself. And maybe for you.

Q. *What is a sacrament?*
A. *A sacrament is an outward sign instituted by Christ to give grace.*

Oho! Another qualification. Could this writing (and reading) give grace? And then the hunt for what *grace* is or can be. It is almost a signal or meter of our reaching or straining for the more. Are we aware of it enough to be thankful, to actually say "thank you," to feel connected to what we reach for? Are we *gracious* enough to be *graceful?* Does this act of writing make me more aware of my reaching and how far I've come and at least a bit of what I'm reaching for? Perhaps we're messing around with power here, with grasp as well as reach. Does this writing out of my thoughts enable them to be clearer, to give my thinking some kind of power, at least over itself?

Speaking of grace, the popular and just about self-righteous expression "There but for the grace of God go I" lays a lot on God. So often, the sight of someone in a sorry state of life provokes the statement. Seeing a disabled beggar on the street, the more fortunate seems kind and so understanding with his "There but for the grace of God go I." But who's to say that the panhandler is not possessed of and by the grace of God? Or who's to say that God has not been at his best work in fashioning the life and circumstance of such a person? Are God's work and presence in me superior to his work and presence in the beggar? Hmmmm. There's presence underneath, throughout, and above this entire writing process. I am present to what I'm trying to express. I am present to my imagined version of you and the disabled indigent. And you are present to the object of my faulty attempts and to your imagination of me at my laptop. How do we explain or imagine such presences, simultaneous, intangible, and everywhere? Well, on God's part, that takes some real spirit. 'Nuff said/written on the Holy Spirit?

All the above seems to be an argument for down-to-earth godliness, almost practical stuff. The most common and holy practice I know, I learned in India. Upon greeting another person of any status or function, a person bows with hands together (thumbs, ahem, uncrossed) and says, "Namaste," fairly assured that the gesture and greeting will be returned. For me, it is just about the most sacred thing two human beings can do. "Namaste" means "I revere the divine in you," hence the bow. Breathtaking, no matter how many times you do it. Somehow "Tsup, dude?" doesn't achieve such intensity.

Oh, the consequences. Given even a modicum of awareness, we walk in holiness. If our hearts and minds are open, we encounter divinity, and we repeat the encounters of Jesus all the time. But so often, anger closes us down to such presences. Unfair judgments of others rob our encounters of anything like a holy presence. Sadly, such judgments are often the residue of faulty religious notions. The energy behind so-called *preaching* can just be publicly vented anger. Pity the many trapped audiences called congregations. Such vented anger in the name of godliness does not only occur in churches or temples.

A few days ago, while boarding a bus, a new passenger tried with her rolling eyes to warn us already seated passengers about the noise being made by another new passenger behind her. The holy noise soon descended upon us. "It is the Holy Ghost that solves our problemsssssuh. He makes things right in the name of Godddduh. Now, hear the word of the Lord in the name of Jesusssssssuh. And I preach in his holy namemuh. And no one can stop me from preaching on this bussssssuh. Because this is the United States and the American Declaration of Independence was based on the Christtttt...uh." Well, you get the, uh, message. But the *uhs* were not just pauses for thought; they were spat out as bass drums of overeager, angry authority. And of course, the entire performance called for an antiphonal response from at least one passenger recalling "life, liberty, and the pursuit of happiness" to call out: "Why aren't you happy...uh?"

But only uncomfortable silence prevailed. We were more isolated from her than from our fellow passengers. Given the lexical meaning of *religion,* "linked, bound with," how sad and irreligious was such isolation.

I am fortunate to have ridden through a substantial portion of my life with more balanced and talented passengers, so many of them Jesuit, members of the Society of Jesus. I have a Jesuit friend, Bill Cain, the award-winning playwright, who describes his experience of God as a penetrating and pervading mystery that settles on him and convinces him of his great individual worth. His so-humble use of the word *mystery* evokes the distinction another Jesuit, Bernard J. Lonergan, makes wherein *myth* indicates that which we don't know we don't know and *mystery* indicates that which we know we don't know. The difference might be expressed as the unknown unknown and the known unknown. Thus, people who deal in myths don't know that they don't know what they're talking about. Those who respect mystery *know* they don't know what they're talking about. It might be *gold, frankincense, and myrrh* vs. the presence that presses me to write and be thankful, loving, and larger than I am. Not so much smelly smoke in the latter (unless this laptop catches fire).

I'm so happy my friend wrote about mystery and stimulated such thinking. Besides Lonergan, he has reminded me of Einstein's famous etude on mystery.

> *The most beautiful thing we can experience is the mysterious. It is the source of all true art and science. He to whom this emotion is a stranger, who can no longer pause to wonder and stand rapt in awe, is as good as dead . . . This insight into the mystery of life, coupled though it be with fear, has also given rise to religion. To know that what is impenetrable to us really exists, manifesting itself as the highest wisdom and most radiant beauty which our dull faculties can comprehend only in the most primitive forms—this knowledge, this feeling, is at the center of true religiousness. In this*

sense, and in this sense only, I belong in the ranks of devoutly religious men. (*Living Philosophies,* Simon and Schuster, 1931, p. 6)

Perhaps Einstein was too humble to realize that his passion to discover a unified field theory was a dramatic impulse to reveal God as a dynamic source of oneness throughout the universe. But that profound sense of unity between apparently contradictory forces must have spoken the deity to him. It must have seemed such an intimate relationship with whatever God is to discover and articulate the deity's power in yet another apparent contradiction. In this, Einstein became a yearning apostle of divine unity. One wishes he could have met the Jesuit poet Gerard Manley Hopkins, if only to discuss the dramatic opening line of the poet's "God's Grandeur": "The world is charged with the grandeur of God."

There is another Jesuit I wish Einstein could have met, another scientist and a contemporary: Pierre Teilhard de Chardin. It is with his concept of *noosphere,* the earth's third stage of evolution after geosphere and biosphere, the stage of consciousness or knowing, that I relate Teilhard to Einstein. Obviously, this is another unification example wherein the deceptive scatter in mankind's thought is seen related to a wholistic concept about existence. Since they died within ten days of each other in 1955, there are clues to existential magnetism even in these deaths. Teilhard prayed successfully that he might die on Easter; Einstein did not pass until he had jotted down a deathbed note.

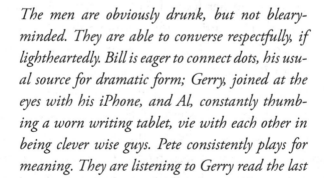

All of the above could set up the ending of a brand-new play: "Albert Einstein and Three Jesuits Walk into a Bar." It would be a very long play, of course, and it would solve many problems over many drinks and through much harmony. In a final exchange, unfocused but endearing, the four would explore the possible meanings of that last writing.

The men are obviously drunk, but not bleary-minded. They are able to converse respectfully, if lightheartedly. Bill is eager to connect dots, his usual source for dramatic form; Gerry, joined at the eyes with his iPhone, and Al, constantly thumbing a worn writing tablet, vie with each other in being clever wise guys. Pete consistently plays for meaning. They are listening to Gerry read the last lines of "God's Grandeur" from his iPhone.

Gerry: "But for all this, nature is never spent—"

Al: *(Cutting in)* Only slightly naïve.

Pete: Only if you're a pessimist.

Bill: C'mon, friends.

Gerry: *(Smiling, continuing)* "Because the Holy Ghost over the bent world broods with warm breast and with ah! Bright wings!"

Al: Nice. Opens with "charged" and ends with "bright." Nice. But *spirits* have wings, not *ghosts*.

Pete: Bill, explain meter to him. He never could count.

It is Al who leads the laughter.

Gerry:: Well it isn't really a question of meter since it's sprung rhythm. Stressed syllables are all that need counting and in fact *spirits* and *ghosts* do have the same number of stressed syllables.

Pete: Well, I don't know about all that but you didn't read my favorite part: "There lives the dearest freshness deep down things."

Al: We've been over this, Pete. That's gravity, not evolution. Though I grant you it *is* providential.

Pete: Thank you.

Bill: *(Checking his watch)* Guys, it's almost 4:30 in the morning. But I have an idea that we should make our last topic.

Gerry: *Deo gratias!*

Al: Ah? What did I teach you? You're too Catholic.

Gerry: *Mea culpa!* Danker Got.

Pete: *(Still brooding over "providential")* I suppose it's what old Al meant with that last scribbling.

Bill: Exactly.

Gerry: What he meant exactly?

Al: Exactly. It just so happens I have it right here *(Passing the tablet around while an image of the note is* unobtrusively *projected onto the set).*

Pete: Well, quite obviously, it's not an equation.

Gerry: *(Staring at his phone's screen)* Sure looks like one to me. How do you know?

Bill: No equal sign.

Al: Exactly. But that doesn't mean it fails to describe something. It just fails to give us another identity for itself.

Pete: So, it thinks it's complete and obvious as it stands? That's crazy.

Al: Exactly. And it couldn't be more complete.

Gerry: Oh, oh! I see where this might be headed. *(To Al)* You've spent your whole life trying to tie everything together. Are we supposed to see this as the ultimate unity?

Al: Well, I don't know if you're *supposed* to, but it can be done.

Pete: How?

Gerry: *(Waving his phone at them)* No, wait, everybody. It's God's email address. I just sent him a message.

Pete: Don't be ridiculous.

Bill: *(Very excited. Reaches for the phone. Reads)* This is amazing.

Pete: And ridiculous.

Gerry: Wait. Wait! A new message: *(Reading)* "Don't *you* be ridiculous, Father de Chardin. I am the ultimate equal sign in all existence. I am."

Bill: *(Humbled. Quiet.)* He. Is.

Pause.

Al: And Pete, Gerry was able to realize this manifestation just because of what you made us realize about ourselves.

Pete: We've already been over this. The internet is not the noosphere.

Gerry: No, but it's a very graphic and functional part of it.

Al: Thank you.

Gerry: Are we to assume that this expression is more than just an email address?

Al: You might.

Gerry: Is it something more intimate about God?

Al: *(Hesitating with emotion)* I think…I think… I sometimes hope so.

Bill: What are all those fractions about?

Gerry: And those letters? *(Looking at iPhone)* It says here they're units of electromagnetic force. And then there are units of gravity that alter. . . *(He has made a connection, and his expression becomes frozen, almost in awe)*

Al: *(Now overwhelmed)* Ex…actly.

The following happens in rapid succession, almost simultaneously

Bill: *(Moving toward the professor)* Al, are you alright?

Pete: We didn't want to upset you.

Bill: *(Offering a glass)* Have some water?

Al: *(Accepting glass)* Thank you so much. *(Drinks and then breaks down completely as he blubbers)* He must be beautiful, but this is all I can get.

Stunned silence. Alarm. Long, sacred silence.

Gerry: *(Oh so cautiously)* Al. Is this the face of God?

Sacred silence.

Al: *(Still very emotional)* I tried so hard. *(Silence)* This was all.

Pete: *(Very cautiously)* What...do you mean, Al?

Al: *(Gradually becoming the teacher)* Those are units of electrical charge expressed as brightness. But the gravity was overpowering and pulled...most of the face *(Very saddened again)* down.

Pause.

Bill: *(Still cautious)* So, are these mathematical expressions of the eyes of God?

Al: No. It is only the light from one eye. All the great Einstein could come up with was the twinkle in God's eye. *(He surprises himself with an awkward laugh)* Can you imagine what Mozart would have done with that? *(Standing to conduct musicians. He has completely recovered from his emotions)* Twinkle, twinkle, little star, how I wonder—

Bill: What—

Pete: You—

Gerry: *(Lost in his wonderment. He has set the phone down)* Are.

Lights.

2

INTEGRITY

TOGETHER, **AS IN** "she has it together." *Whole,* as in "whole number," which is an *integer* for our friend Albert.

Socially, integrity becomes evident in the consistency with which a person interacts with others, no matter the occasion. Individually, a person senses her integrity when all of her functions can be counted on consistently. They are harmonious, and she doesn't surprise herself very often. She knows who and what she is.

Political integrity demands that a social body avoid differing ethical codes regardless of minor situational differences: if it's wrong, it's wrong. It takes an application of a higher level of integrity for circumstances to modify a code.

With personal, social, or political integrity, you not only get what you see, but you get what you give as well, and you're not surprised. The result is not at all boredom, but the confidence to plan and build so that a social unit expands and strengthens.

Corruption can occur with mistaken perceptions about what it takes to be *whole*. Integrity is compromised by false promises or what are perceived as promises. The guarantees of false advertising for better income, sensational good looks, or immediate social acceptance are among the most common threats to integrity.

Conversely, strength and sound growth occurs when *wholeness* can be perceived as one's ability and privilege. This often hinges on a keen sense of the difference between *need* and *want,* a lesson most of us cry to be taught at a very early age.

Honesty goes a long way to building and protecting integrity. I would not be a writer of integrity if I let you go through that first chapter thinking I know very much about Einstein's equations. I know nothing about them except the famous $E = mc^2$ and the areas of interest the equations serve. Nor am I completely up on Chardin's theories. Poetry and literature are my background, so I can give dear Hopkins a fair shake.

I am a clown, and I have been from a childhood of backyard circuses through twenty-eight years of touring with professional circuses. The only thing dishonest about circus clowning is the makeup, which everyone knows is unreal. But whether you see his face or not, a clown still falls down, his pants still fall down, and he still gets doused with water. He still is "just" a clown amid the acrobatic poetry in motion. So, pretense is not part of my usual bag.

Except when I do magic. I practiced all the usual tricks from my boyhood and always incorporated them into my concept of circus entertainment. But rabbits from hats and impressive card predictions take place in the context of entertainment, not the spooky-spooky world of séance or crystal balls. Long ago, we learned that there are no real clowns or magicians, only actors playing the roles of clowns and magicians, and few of such actors lose themselves—and their integrity—to the point of actually believing they are clowns and/or magicians. Of course, they must believe in what they're doing to the degree that the audience will swallow the illusion, but then the spotlights go down, the makeup comes off, the rabbits go back into their cages, and everyone goes to dinner. Professional lying must keep strict hours, or integrity can wear thin.

There are wonderful advantages to being whole, to having it together. And there are clues. Such integrity most often overrules anything like bashfulness. Eyes can meet eyes, as in "He always looks you in the eye no matter what he's talking about." That's because such people have long since evaluated all the aspects of their personality and found them good, or at least acceptable. Stuff just doesn't get hidden. Sometimes when inherited body parts, including brains and nervous systems, seem to dictate seclusion, such personalities can develop an integrity that appropriates even their unusual behaviors as their own. Then they can walk, limp, or roll through life with a near-statuesque strength that usually becomes beautiful.

It is a mark of integral achievement when a society comes to value the personal strength found in citizens completely aware of themselves. The signs of such achievement are manifest in focus on early value-centered education, remedial tutoring, widespread hunger relief, and the physical and psychological tutoring required by special needs. The word *disability* might become irrelevant since an integrated personality would simply, matter-of-factly name the special situation of their life, indicating strength and the need to educate listeners. After all, personality derives its value from unicity or individuality. Many of us are just different or unique in different ways. I'm bald, and you could kick a field goal between my two front teeth. There were times when I regretted hair loss and looked with interest at ads for orthodontics, but then I learned to accept all of myself, and life was less stressful. Hey, I'm me. Of course, it helps to have a strong awareness of what you have achieved and can still achieve. And that's where an effective, complete—integral—education becomes so helpful.

A perceived approach to a recognized need is so promising because self-hidden shortcomings and ignored needs never get addressed or accommodated enough to enjoy resolution. And such resolution does bring joy, the joy of meeting another personality while confident that the reciprocal experience is rich and worthwhile. "I am worth your being introduced to me." That is the goal for all of us, and the very acceptance of such a goal is a measure toward reaching it.

Given a majority of such honest confidence everywhere in society, the possibility of genuine and transparent leadership becomes real. With that, special needs everywhere are approached productively in what has long been thought of as *common wealth*.

Easier written than done. Only hours after writing the above paragraphs, there was a knock at my door. As a rule, if I don't know you're coming, I don't answer the door. But I was putting on a jacket to go out anyway. I had a good idea who was knocking because he had told me he had been looking for me. I also had a good idea about why he was looking for me. It was the end of the month. Sure 'nuff. A quiet tête-à-tête in the hallway got right to the point: "Can you loan me ten dollars till next Wednesday?"

I live with many neighbors who waltz "check to check" with social security. But some are not keen enough with their budgeting to actually get from check to check, so they need extra help, such as the food pantries, stock boxes, and outright community gifts of fresh vegetables and meat. Alas, there's no help with booze, smokes, or lottery tickets, and my friend in the hallway made no effort to hide his struggle with all three of those questionable habits. So, I lied to him. "No, man, I can't. I'm broke, too. Payday to payday, you know!" All that with a loose twenty-dollar bill in my pocket.

Complicating the scene was the fact that he knew I used to be a priest, and thought I still was. (No matter how many times I tell the story and try to explain *laicization,* people can't seem to shake the echoes of "thou are a priest forever according to the order of Melchizedek.") So, maybe he thought I was endlessly honest and charitable. Hey, I'd like to be! I lack the integrity to worry about whether he noticed I couldn't completely meet his eyes. Did he know I was lying? I also caught myself recess-wondering whether there were mitigating factors to get me off the hook. Was this just a mental reservation, as in "No, I can't" (understood: "loan YOU anything because the doctor has warned you about impairing your health with these bad habits")? It wouldn't work, so I lied about being broke.

The more subtle failure in integrity is to worry about my image. Such a two-dimensional concern with self is fractured, not whole. There's a part of me that is a liar. Still. Even off the stage or out of the circus ring. Accept it. Why was it so impossible to just say no and explain my concerns? Would it have been so tough to explain that I was refusing him out of friendship? But would he believe I really do think of him as a friend? He didn't come to me for a lecture but for cash. And I'm sure he went to someone else for that.

So what? I'm a liar, and part of the proof is that I'm so concerned about whether he knew it. I'm a liar, and I just had a fine challenge to my own perceived integrity. Will I appropriate all this as who I am and proceed with the wholeness I have?

And if all these questions can be asked and struggled with and lied about in the dimly lit hallways of a HUD senior residence, what questions, struggles, and lies transpire in the bright corridors of our capitols, legislatures, and judiciaries? Political integrity is as difficult as it is rare, so it should evoke little surprise that our so-called societies are not integrated. Our urban populations, in particular, exhibit dramatic scenes of disintegration.

I am writing in the most segregated city in our nation. The "'hood" is a recognized point of reference on city maps and in the memories of all who have been there. And while I have neighbors who talk about their relief at being out of the hood, there are others for whom being from the hood remains a point of strength, precisely because another sector of society (e.g., mine) doesn't know how mean and nasty the mf's in the hood can be. This seems a type of celebratory decay. Not only fear and ignorance produce such resistance, but the perceived absence of any advantage to melding with the majority sectors of society.

"What do those sectors exhibit that is better than what we have?"

Oh, c'mon. Isn't it obvious that the reduced traffic in drugs, nights free of neighborhood gunfire, and safe streets for children would be preferable to the opposite?

Such a brave question from a crib such as mine teases a very complicated answer. Immediately I sense that whatever I think or say comes from a position of power I take for granted. It's base? A history of like control and power. And the foundation of basic control and power? Is it economic? Is just about everything better about where I live a result of there being more available money than where you live? Or do I have a higher chance of getting employment and a better job than you? Or is my network (read: schools, churches, stores, jobs, neighborhood councils) one that joins me to more avenues of wealth than yours does? Or, in contrast, when I do approach possible avenues of power, do I routinely hang my head, avoid eye contact, shuffle my feet? Am I a loser from the start?

Okay, it's circular, and it's not a circus ring. I can be born into non-achievement and immediately contract the behaviors and attitudes of losing. And that's what I'll assume about others in my situation, and perhaps even teach them: a dark congeries of expectations, self-limiting in every sense.

In such a discussion, skin color and perceivable racial difference become pertinent, especially when you are riding the bus with a black person dressed in a suit and obviously professional for more reasons than that he carries a fine leather briefcase. As soon as you speak to him, you can tell that he is quite American, not African. He is a Cubs fan and teaches in the sociology department at a university. In conversation, he can even outpace you in an academic level of discussion that soon gets to the brass tacks of his pet project: getting black kids out of the circular trap of the hood.

Regardless of our social status and background, do most of us move through our regular personal environments with a sense of wholeness? Are we free of needed cautions because there is nothing but integrity in the way our personal lives are protected and supported? Or do we move inside a clunky complex of attitudinal armor because we need to be on guard against system failures? From property managers, landlords, and realtors, through aldermen, city supervisors, state assembly personnel, and state senators, and all the way to a given governor's apparatus, we are subject to the vagaries of political support. In any one of the ten or so offices just listed, what is the primary motivating factor behind any decision on behalf of constituents? Is it fear of appearing weak or of not being impressive enough to merit a promotion? Or is it truly a decision enabling any or many constituents to be safe, prosperous, and supported by their social and economic contexts? Do I, as a citizen of this state, feel integral with the power points of the state's chain of command because I am certain the state is supporting me in every way? Or do I even let the state know who I am by voting or campaigning?

I live in an apartment among thirteen floors of like apartments. Our population is a surprising collection of immigrant Ukrainians, Belarusians, Russians, and Americans who are black, white, and represent all levels of education and professionalism. As a matter of faith, we are Jewish, practicing Protestant, and Catholic, and there are more fallen-away than you can shake a candlestick at. Probably the only thing that holds us together is the building itself because such a disparate group of about ninety people does not enjoy the representation of a residents' council or even a suggestion box. Changes and hoped-for improvements come from an administration that, at best, has asked tenants what they think via the occasional and impersonal questionnaire. But most policy modification comes exclusively from the top because the avenues of interchange are quite limited. We aren't an integrated residential community. The problem might be fear of the amount of complaint that would register if there were community sounding boards and pathways of communication. Fear so often shatters what fragile integrity an individual can manage personally and socially. Do I feel integrated enough to formally propose to management a carefully worked-out (written) suggestion on policy?

The ramifications of mutual integrity between state and constituents, citizens and local administrators are significant. It is not enough to have personal convictions, no matter how well reasoned. Everyone else, whether governing or governed, must share in those convictions at least to the point of knowing what they are. Such sharing is heavily dependent upon conversation of all types and on all levels. The adage that "We don't talk politics or religion here" no longer leaves just the weather to bore ourselves with. Weather is now political, and if that is not known, there hasn't been enough conversation. How we think and feel about the policies that govern our lives cry out to be heard. Politeness does not excuse such conversation. An

Athenian during the fourth or fifth century BCE could have recognized his own words for *city, politics, policy,* and even *police* in our seemingly effete *polite.* This is not just etymological hubris. All of these connected nouns unite in their efforts to ensure consistency and mutual support—*integrity*—in a city-state. So, let's whip that into the turkey dressing next Thanksgiving even if it only gets us through a discussion of whether we should worry about the weather in grandmother's woods. Talk is cheap; not talking can get expensive.

As it happens, there is a local election coming up soon. Thanks to a public conversation in the press, I know enough to vote consistently based on the conversations I've had about the issues and candidates. But I don't feel voting and discussion is enough. Some of my neighbors are helping at the polls; others attend public meetings. I am not convinced that waiting for the big noises of national rallies, speeches, and elections is even as effective as involvement at the more local level, with its quieter events. There is some personal growth needed here.

Where? Two paragraphs back!

In the senior community residence that is my home, there is no effort to get our non-ambulatory residents to the polling place, which is right around the corner. Nor is there any encouragement to use absentee ballots. I have thought about this long enough. It's time to make a formal approach laced with practical proposals and backed with examples from other, similar residences. It may take some doing because there could be some conflict of interest waiting to rear its head: our building is owned and managed by Baptist Housing Ministries, and most of our tenants receive rent subsidies from the United States Department of Housing and Urban Development.

But here's my effort toward political integrity.

The following letter will be presented to local administrarors and it will be mailed to regional authorities of the Baptist Housing Ministries on the same day. Care has been taken to forestall conflict of interest concerns and the community's lack of interest.

DATE:

RE:

To Whom It May Concern:
The spring primary elections will be held in Milwaukee on February 18, 2020. Judging from reactions in the past, there will be at Cambridge Senior Apartments little interest or concern, or

even voiced plans, to vote. In my thirteen years here, my impression is that involvement in the democratic process is a non-issue, much like the positions and propositions being voted on. Yet there is political interest and, indeed, a bit of passion on both sides of the major political divide, judging from the hours of the Fox News channel available as well as copies of the liberal Shepherd Express in the building.

My concern is whether this lack of participation in our important democratic rights might be remedied. Can the community—or a significant part of it—be stimulated to see their rights as requiring protection? Might the privileges we enjoy as citizens be understood as concomitant with our duty to safeguard them? Can we be stimulated to a higher degree of political involvement than just rednecks and lefties verbally duking it out in front of the community television monitor? Can such exchanges be challenged to put ballots where mouths are?

I think so.

Awareness of elections and the issues they address are paramount. At least a month ahead of time, there must be some effort to stimulate concerns, even over school boards and local judges. Efforts must be mustered to alert the community to how such issues affect us and our children, grand-children, and other loved ones. Just because we might not be touched personally by election out-comes does not mean those we care about won't be. In other words, the education must be personal.

Who should orchestrate such an education? No one on campus. There would be too much sus-picion of bias and lack of expertise to allow any of the community an effective platform. Who, then? There have to be more than a few political scien-tists—even political science students—who would be willing to organize a presentation tailored to the needs and concerns of Cambridge residents. Such an orientation would include the actual ballots (available in advance online) that will be used in our district. A stipend could be modest if any is expected, and contacts with the academic communities in the area should not be difficult.

It is almost proverbial at Cambridge that some will not attend any public event unless there are free snacks provided. What I am proposing is a seasonal effort to awaken awareness. It would not at all be as regular as movie nights or bingo. A budget for light food and drink on such occasions should be feasible. This is an attempt to bring our residents into contact with professional stimula-tion to vote and to vote responsibly. Speakers should be briefed and prepared to counter such mindsets as total indifference to politics or completely set opinions that resist any informational effort to enlighten.

But motivation is just the beginning. Completing and submitting ballots is the goal. First of all, copies of the ballots should be downloaded and posted on the community bulletin board and made available at the service coordinator's kiosk. But several degrees of ambulatory skill obtain in the building, including the need for wheelchairs, walkers, and canes. Certainly as much effort could be made to transport these neighbors to the polls as is made in getting them to weekly shopping destinations. Short of personal voting, absentee ballots and instructions on how and when to use them can be given in-house with follow-up to see that they are completed. May I suggest that contact be made with Milwaukee Catholic Home to learn how that administration provides easy access to absentee ballots for its residents.

It would also be very important to post the election results, perhaps even using the advanced ballots. Why play if there's a chance you'll miss the score?

Finally, it must be said that of late, there have

been efforts to keep us informed of elections and deadlines. This has been done via "day of" bulletin board announcements and election dates noted in the monthly calendars. Details and issues, however, have not been brought home to the community, nor has there been a recognized effort to transport would-be voters or instruct those needing absentee ballots.

In no way is this letter meant to stir up political or administrative ire. Nor does it seem an avenue toward conflict of interest, since the primary educational efforts are to be academic. My purpose is to help talkers become voters and "by-sitters" become participants.

Sent with my best regards.

To the polls on Republic Day, India

3

SEX

WELL, OF COURSE there's a chapter on sex. Sex sells. Everything. Even itself. Indeed, its stores of intriguing merchandise may have sated us to the point where we have little interest.

[*Disclaimer: This writer is fully aware that writing on such a subject as an eighty-year-old lifetime bachelor incurs a risk of seriously limited data and potential bias toward the subject. But oh, the memories and imaginings. Bring on recess!*]

The application of the word *romantic* reflected in the art of a given time seems to be a marker, indeed a zenith, for the real power of sex, and yet discussions of that eighteenth-to-nineteenth century phenomenon usually circumvent the sexual. The notion of sublimation seems too cold a description of what is happening

in the alignment of human attraction and sexual arousal. There is a charge of emotion, a thrust in the use of
realism that indulges all of our senses. It is as if the synapses and neuronic connections in today's ubiquitous
discussions are not only at recess. They may be at gym
class. And with few exceptions triggered by explicit
physicality, the force of such art is seldom attributed
to the power of sex when it is seamlessly present in the
power of love. Great sex is romantic.

Realism run riot in the modern and post-modern
way of life has rendered the connection between romance and sexual love anything but seamless. As with
everything else, control is prime, so the ease of "on-
off," "in-out," and "set it for later" must be applied
even to the species-preserving dynamo urge within us.
In that we know when we are in control and what is
controlling us when we're not in control, these are good
reflexes. But in that they separate sex from the human
capacity for romantic love, perhaps they're not so good.

So much of the power of romantic love is in the
surprise with which it happens. Guards are down, and
we have no idea what attraction waits "across a crowded room" in the eyes of a stranger on "some enchanted
evening." There is no preparation for such a lurch of
power, even if we went to a "nice" school where we
can meet a "nice" boy or girl and live "nicely" in the
plans of Mother and Father. Similarly, we might not

have obeyed a sister's admonition, "Stick to your own kind," in finding another race, culture, or family attractive. And of course, such themes abound in Western literature, back through Shakespeare to Sophocles. I find such a phenomenon significant in both its energy and its relegation of sex to a minor role, if not a back seat, so to speak. Because, the truth is, love begins from the neck up, and the brain is like Command Central, ordering around the isolated barracks of the groin and scattered erectile tissue. If in a pansexual culture like ours, even a meeting of eyes translates to a promise of intense sexual contact, do we know we're shortchanged? Not only have we missed the warmth of romantic enchantment, but that very sexual contact just might not be so intense.

"Where's so-and-so?"

"Where do you think? Down to a bar to see if he can pick up a chick."

Enter "appliance dial/on-off" use of sex. There isn't much mental mileage between a bar "pick-up" and a street corner "pick-up." Both situations cost money; both shortchange the customer in terms of powerful passion. Neither engage complete human beings. Sex itself has been raped.

"Wanna hear a good dirty joke?"

Such an overture cries out for translation of language and thought. Undoubtedly, *dirty* is the common code for *sexual*. *Good* simply means *very funny*. And if the addressee does want to hear the joke, it suggests that both parties are of the widespread culture that considers sex to be dirty, very impolite, improper. And funny. Because, truth be told, sex is the biggest joke played on our species! Or is it?

What probably makes sex so rich a mine for humor is that jokes about it make those oh-so-private matters doff their covers. We have so long and so carefully covered up our bodies that nudity itself can become comic. The adage "If God had meant for us to run around naked we would have been born that way!" tells all. To be fair to modesty, though, eons ago, our hair and fur gave way to newly achieved artificial coverings so that skin eventually became as endangered by exposure as it was beautiful. But the key component in our shyness might be that the same body vents that eject our waste emit our vital fertile materials, and indeed ourselves. So, what are we trying to hide? Maybe both sets of functions. And because they share the privacy we afford them, they also share in the attributes we give them. So, sex—and everything *down there*—becomes *dirty*.

The female chest is not an entirely different story since some of the same synapses seem to be traveled during the stimulation of suction. So, at least nipples become covered or play peek-a-boo with folks seeking arousal of parts farther south in the anatomy. That's sorta funny in itself.

"Bless me, Father, for I have sinned. It has been one week since my last confession, and I told a dirty joke."

I was seven years old, and my confessor was a very nice Irishman sitting on his side of the gloomy contraption called a confessional.

"What do you mean by 'dirty'?"

"Well, it's about this lady who is told by her doctor that she can't eat peas for forty years. So, at the end of the forty years, she gives a huge banquet, including a very big bowl of green peas, and invites all her friends. Before they take a bite, she raises a toast: 'My friends, this is the first pea I've had in forty years.' A man at the other end of the table shouts, 'Everybody who can't swim, head for the chandeliers!'"

I laughed out loud on my side of the confessional booth, exposing my lack of contrition. I can't imagine Father Doheny wasn't laughing as well. That's all I can recall of the episode, but I am confident that I wasn't allowed to go away thinking I'd done something immoral. I was just very young.

Given that humor really does result from the juxtaposition of opposites, it could be helpful to identify the opposing objects or attitudes that obtain when we laugh about sex. Basically, we seem to hold ourselves above sex and anything else that evokes our animal ancestry. We've passed significantly beyond the apes—thank you very much and tut-tut—in our need to procreate. Even Shakespeare taught us that in his writings of four centuries ago when he had comics belittle heavy human flirtation with the mocking "Goats and monkeys! Goats and monkeys!" So, when there is a sudden shift in which humans are at least implicitly revealed as earlier on the evolutionary trail, our "tut-tut" is juxtaposed with a "grunt-grunt" or two, and it's funny.

Disrespectful as it seems, laughter around matters of sex may be far more healthy than blushing-red silence. Not speaking or referring to sexual matters might seem proper. After all, we call our sex organs *privates*. But you don't need a graduate degree in psychology to recognize the effects of so-called repression. It is very dangerous to artificially contain such a powerful component of humanity. And if the majority of nitty-gritty sex education is from juvenile peers, how much of a chance is there that balanced and mature attitudes will develop? Might sex then always be a dirty joke?

For almost two millennia, a major dimension of sexual development escaped public attention and gave sporadic rise to a cruel crudity both in humor and general behavior: homosexuality. Fortunately, during the 1950s, there were "eyes open" and more-or-less scientific examinations of the phenomenon. While both the Kinsey and the Masters and Johnson studies are highly criticized, the publicity they received at least cut through the dodgy silence surrounding the subject. Minimally, society knew for sure that there were enough instances of same-sex attraction to merit academic discussion. Whether there was yet a scientific explanation is doubtful. It is certain, though, that the reaction to these protean examinations led to brusque efforts to change orientations (Masters and Johnson) and politically resist them. Ten years after Masters and Johnson, the repression attempts exploded at Stonewall in New York City. The rest is a history of both respectable and irreverent attention-calling to overcome the dangerous silence.

The causes of same-sex preference seem to be multiple and both biological and social. But until we better understand the function the brain plays in the womb through the embryonic and fetal states, there will not be definitive science on the subject. Besides, silent shame seems certain to be controlling the populations available for study.

My neighborhood has played host to at least three transsexuals. Probably less is known about such psychology than about homosexuality, and what studies there are will likely favor post-natal influences and active choice over biological determination. But here, again, there is evidence of the brain's contribution to the developing embryo and fetus, as Amy Ellis Nutt makes clear in her detailed case study *On Becoming Nicole* (New York: Random House, 2015).

The sensational, at least half-embarrassed atmosphere in which these matters get their limited airings forestalls straightforward science and even humanistic appreciation. There is a willful blindness toward what appear to be nature's exceptions, to the extent that many "ordinary" folks live their lives oblivious to the contributions made to society by our gay and transsexual brothers and sisters. One wonders where theater, dance, and painting would be without gay contributors. For that matter, the populations of truck drivers, mechanics, and psychologists would shrink.

Frightfully, the most significant effects of our awareness of homosexuality seem the dangerous ones that brand the condition illegal and punishable, and religious conservatives who eschew it as immoral. A neighbor of mine, Baptist by religion, recently called an openly gay neighbor "an abomination." Such pronouncements always drive us to the book of Leviticus (the gay guy doesn't *look* like a Levite!), the manual of Bible-thumpers who enjoy condemnations. Sure 'nuff! Chapter 18, verse 22. But wait! Our Baptist neighbor was wearing Levi's and a cotton knit t-shirt and polyester cap. Chapter 19, verse 19 forbids the wearing of more than one fabric at a time. By the time such a discussion gets to the blessed selling of one's daughter into slavery, we had better get the point: we ain't Levites, and Yahweh doesn't legislate for the twenty-first century through desert dreams.

And just as we wonder how social life might be if the players in this game of sex would "just leave each other alone," we happen upon a gift, that giant of a question among all others: What really matters anyway? And that gift, heavily flirting with indifference, seems to be enjoyed by current generations, who even see sex as a potential distraction to their need for human love. Sex seems noisy; love quiet. The often drunken body-brawl holds sex cheap; love is precious and guarded like a diamond. Why? Is God love?

It could be that an important and illustrative balance is to be found in our society's concern for sexual safety. The public advertising of condoms and the availability of HIV testing is an example. Sexual protection is not seen as sinful but a deterrent from disease. (Yes, couples desiring a child know that pregnancy is a blessed gift and not a disease. Joke over.) The lethal phenomenon of AIDS teaches us that as human life perdures, there are new lessons, new adventures to encounter and survive. "Is it worth the trouble?" we ask the folks in love. And how often it is the exceptional or unusual situation that proves most powerful in teaching us the important chapters in life.

Two women I know were partners long enough to realize they wanted to marry, and moving to a Pacific island, they wed in a ceremony that included one lover's daughter. In the course of the ceremony,

*Romantic and sacred art on Chandela
temple in Khajuraho, India*

A closer view. Still sacred.

after the exchange of rings, the blessed couple turned and presented their daughter with a ring. There it is. Love makes us one. (I made sure Einstein was on their minds. You see, he and I have been going to bars for a long time.) For their wedding, I sent them a poem.

Janice, Jodie, and Einstein walk into a bar.
(Though "fetched," this is anything but "far.")
Albert thinks the ladies have provided the light
That might bring his unified field theory closer
    to sight.
Their insights may complement his thinking,
And that gifted opportunity calls for drinking.

Just when most energies seem all over the field
And matter and minds no unity will yield,
As nations and parties, even earth and air,
Clash to the point where all despair,
There blossoms anew in the mid-Pacific
Witness to a fusion nothing short of terrific.
Where West meets East and both disappear,
Janice and Jodie lock in a bond most dear
And fuse their energies for a life anew,
Rejecting factions driving all askew.
Here in human love's mighty surprise,
Albert finds forceful power that unifies.

Here is promise: oneness answers a yearning
Built into all and in all nearly burning.
Inside unity is new and stronger being,
The chance for clearer and brighter seeing.
That's the wisdom in love's tough hold;
It renders less more and the fearful bold.

Not one person observing this unlikely trio
Knows the old man's thoughts now play *con brio*
Till Albert raises the toast: "Here's to your love,
With thanks for your celebration thereof,
Brave witness to humanity's force most strong,
And to charged happiness your whole lives long."

A sublime contradiction is that for all the brou-
haha from whatever corners of society, today's attitude so often echoes with "It's no big deal." And it
isn't, to continue with the satiety remark opening this
chapter.

Society's younger echelons have, in particular,
found sex's place in their lives, and there it remains with
all its smoke and raging mirrors. Life goes on. Like so
much else, "No big deal."

That is, until love raises its bright-eyed head and
after equally bright eyes exchange their magic and blur
their way to a conjured bliss without smoke and mirrors. Unsummoned, sex, now graceful, emerges from

its place and just about ratifies what those eyes began. Just about. For there is always the risk that blurred eyes will drive too fast and the lovers will collide without union or unity. Anger and confusion will then fill the air with blame. If the eyes clear and decide it's worth another try, it will be some time. This "on-off" rhythm may obtain through a few brighter and wiser encounters before there is a new gift of union for some part of society to celebrate. Once again, sex will have found its place. More or less happily.

It may be objected that such a depiction of love and sex mechanizes them both to the extent that the spontaneity of each is unaccounted for. Watch the eyes throughout the story. Are they clear or blurry? (Of course, several senses, feelings, and perceptions comprise the experience of vagueness and the fogging in any human project.) The blessing of "I can't see straight" is that we cannot render what is still an exciting and risky problem as the dull right side of an even duller equation. There is too much of the known unknown, the mysterious, for that.

Perhaps the finest literary instance of not seeing straight occurs in the aubade of Shakespeare's *Romeo and Juliet* after we know that Romeo will be executed if he isn't out of town by dawn. Still in their marriage bed, upon waking, they fight over whether it is dawn and which of the birds' callings they have heard. That their poetic banter isn't all playful might be found in Romeo's willingness to lose his life: "Let me be ta'en; let me be put to death." (3.5.17)

Juliet
Wilt thou be gone? It is not yet near day.
It was the nightingale, and not the lark
That pierced the fearful hollow of thine ear.
Nightly she sings in yond pomegranate tree. (1–4)

Why a pomegranate tree? Always suspect Shakespeare of having layered meanings. The ancient Greeks understood the pomegranate as a symbol of marriage and new life. But the first spat continues.

Romeo
It was the lark, the herald of the morn,
No nightingale. Look, love, what envious streaks
Do lace the severing clouds in yonder east.
Night's candles are burnt out, and jocund day
Stands tiptoe on the misty mountain-tops.
I must be gone and live or stay and die. (6–11)

Of course, it really is a life-and-death matter because Romeo has been banished from Verona for killing Juliet's cousin. More, the Elizabethan second meaning for *die* gets abundant shady (?) exercise in this play above all the others. When Shakespeare's audience heard *die*, it so often referred to an orgasm. Romeo will likely die in one of those ways if he stays in the city. Yet his lover persists.

Juliet
Yond light is not daylight, I know it, I.
It is some meteor that the sun exhaled
To be to thee this night a torchbearer
And light thee on thy way to Mantua
Therefore stay yet. Thou need'st not to be gone.
 (12–16)

Is she seeing straight? Is he? He finally agrees that it is still night and that he will stay and die.

Let me be ta'en; let me be put to death.
I am content, so thou wilt have it so.
....
....
I have more care to stay than will to go.
Come death and welcome. Juliet wills it so. *(17–18; 23–24)*

It is then that she focuses on the reality of their situation. "Oh now begone. More light and light it grows" (35).

4

YOU

> "The first thing you need to know about
> yourself is that you are not a story."
> (Y.N. Harari, *21 Lessons for the 21st Century*,
> NY, Spiegel and Grau, 2018, p. 306)

STILL THERE? DID I lose you? No? Good! Yes? Bad!
I have to get you back.

Truth is, there is no writing without you. Trouble
is, I can only guess who you are: what you like, hate,
need, or want. If I guess wrong, I lose you. If I guess
right, then maybe something worthwhile can appear
on these pages. The project is all about you. But so
much of the "you" hovering over this keyboard is my
projection of myself. And that is grand, the active celebration of human unity. Music. But when the words

fail to connect with your self-identity, there can be fire-works if you're angered—more music should I prompt you to wonder your way to a different part of you.

Publicly and more objectively, everybody is "you." (Only the more sensitive cultures distinguish between the intimate and familial yous and those who are some-what distant, for example, the *tu* and *usted* of Spanish.) So it is that "How do you do?" is made to suit the com-plete stranger and "How are you feeling this morning, sweetheart?" has to suffice for the mate. But in depth, it's really all about me. I can only imagine from my own experiences what constitutes your presence, your pain, your delight.

Except when it comes to your appearance. I wouldn't wish mine on anyone, but mercifully, nature has given us markers. It's easy to tell which who each "you" is. And what are obvious choices about dress and personal fashion gives my you clues as to yours. Even here, though, what you intend with that hair-style bounces off my own judgment and experience with hair; similarly, your choice of shirts and skirts—or pants. Your you can't get away from mine.

The fallout from this near-circular reference mech-anism may be the basis for civilization. Groupings, associations of all kinds, have resulted from the recog-nition of unity amid so much variety. In a group, the individual recognizes something of herself in others, and they in her. Recent historical events have only increased the size of groups and societies that recognize themselves in each other. One wonders if all the emphasis on global unity could have happened without near-global war. Did war achieve what the Bible couldn't? Why are you so engaged by the welfare and struggle of a large Syrian family that has just moved to a neighborhood near you?

If you were still teaching, how are you sure you would not break down at the sight of your Muslim students wearing their hijabs?

And who are you? I notice the care in your wardrobe, the steady eye contact and slight smile. Confidence. Because of my own reflections, I know that underneath those markers are myriad algorithms and near-algorithms of attractions, repulsions, joy, potential rage, prejudice, and rationality, all vying to undergird a productive person. And the brain keeps the algorithms whirling as they mesh or modify at the onset of constantly new data. Or conversely, can I see in a dullness of eye an overload of carelessness, surrender, and social rejection? I have experienced those moods and modes as well. Who are you?

Say you've arrived for your routine examination and cleaning at the dental school. Your turn in the check-in line comes, and the following exchange demands your attention.

"Last name?"

"Trenton"

"First name?"

"Bill. William."

"Date of birth ?"

"Ten. Eighteen. Forty."

"Thank you, Mr. Trenton. You may have a seat."

Well, that may get your teeth cleaned, but it is far from an interpersonal experience. The objection "But we don't expect an *interpersonal experience* in such situations" is well taken. However, such machine-like encounters harden us to the much softer atmosphere that must surround persons and personalities. How long before we treat all encounters like such clockwork.

There might be something beneficial in a slightly adjusted approach.

Before she starts, interrupt her rhythm with a very loud, smiling, and sincere "Good morning!" or even "You mean I have to start before I even get a 'Good morning'?" If she relaxes a bit, there's some hope. Try, after the "date of birth" probe, "Oh, but then you'll know how old I am!" Oh well, it helps to be a clown. Sometimes.

The truth is you are not identifying yourself at all with answers to such file-search questions. You might as well play the game as though you were Walt Disney.

"Last name?"

"Mouse."

"First?"

"Mickey."

"Uh, would that be 'Michael'?"

"No. 'Mickey,' just like it sounds."

"Date of birth?"

"Nine. Eighteen. Twenty-eight."

I'm not sure about the uppers, but I know Mickey has no lower teeth to worry about.

Truth be told, I can barely keep up with who I am, much less enjoy a ready-to-go take on who you are. None of us—and that includes you—is still or finished. Identity is no more a set history than it is the three search items the dental receptionist wants. Each of us is a work in process. Always. So, whenever you and I meet, it's the first time both processes have engaged at this precise point in their ongoing historics. We feed both of them new data while we are together. And because the wonderful music we make together at this meeting must engage much more data before the next time we meet, we will be new musicians on that occasion.

One of the chief obstructions to my having a successful encounter with you might be your failure to accept who and what you are at our meeting. While I must be willing to take what I get, you must be willing to accept and present who you are at the moment. If you try to hide something or lie in any way, the result could be a disaster. My sensing that you are not completely present to me would only breed fear of whatever it is you fear to reveal. And should I fear anything about you, I will, in turn, hide some measure of whoever I am at the moment.

We have to appropriate the process of self as good in itself. At its best, it is art at work; at its worst, it can only spill some paint or bad notes: ill will or pettiness. Once there is confidence in the process itself, we are ready to stand on two feet and confidently share who we are. Certainly, this takes time, and the pace at which present-day society gallops over our more delicate functions seldom allows for relaxed-but-confident presentations of self.

Our most fundamental conviction should be that just having the opportunity to exist is paramount. Existence itself is good and more important than what kind of stuff exists, including us. We are. And *that* we are is good. That understanding should embolden us to accept ourselves as good and worth sharing. Such doctrine is as old as Aristotle, revived by the likes of Soren Kierkegaard and Friedrich Nietzsche, all of them aware they were touching on the holy with such a notion. That is, when you approach me, I sense that I am in the presence of a new instance of being, of existence, shaped uniquely by the process that is you. Heavy stuff no matter what diet you're on, but true.

I need you. That's why I've spent all this time rehearsing what would make you a better you. It's really selfish, but I happen to love myself. Most of the time. Encounters with the likes of you can only make my self-acceptance stronger. Then you get a better me and...and...and...

What happens if all of this backfires? What if you are physically disfigured, convinced that everyone seeing you is disgusted and anxious to get away, and this makes you fearful, at times hateful? Or what if you're somehow psychologically paralyzed and cannot agree with anything anyone puts forward in conversation? Then you try out for a community theater production of Jean-Paul Sartre's play *No Exit*, hoping to get the part of Joseph Garcin so you can publicly say, "Hell is other people," every night.

What if there is no backfire but it all leads to a better you? Then you are John Merrick hearing Mrs. Kendal say, "Oh, Mr. Merrick, you're not the 'Elephant Man'; you're Romeo."

You have power. I found this out last night when a neighbor with whom I have only made comic music before went out into a winter storm to shop at the corner store. We are about as unlike in the way we process life as I can imagine, but I have admired the way his own process has led him through a series of improvements and increased self-esteem. I have increased the amount of attention I pay him, and last night, I was very concerned that he get back safely before dark. A very simple and common concern between individuals. The truth is that I had never even imagined that our relationship could be such a charged process. He increased my own self-esteem. Powerful.

A suspicion has grown in me that the effectiveness of any democratic method of government presumes such empowered processes. Rather than the power of bare politics, the basis of such processes is the compelling "you" in relationship after relationship that cries out for organization, orientation, and protection. This is the root energy that enables a social entity: not the lonesome "I" but the compelling "you." Such altruism cannot help but concretize the reality of a political body. It would be this understanding of the political process that climbs beyond frigid majorities to flesh-and-blood social concern. That concern proves powerful. If a political body is deemed valuable, important, and functional, then the efforts it takes to mutually encourage political activity, e.g., voting and campaigning, make sense. But such activity must always be valued as human, as "you-oriented," wherein the dynamics of the processes that are "you" are preferred over other less human ones. Then there is a chance you might discover more of the truth of another "you" or two. Yes, there might be a modification on both sides.

How much I learn from you. Of course, I start out presuming we are alike and find myself challenged by the dramatic misalignments in our respective wants and needs. Nothing wrong with discovering other ways to do things, other feelings to have about people. Nothing wrong with growth. Perhaps the best teachers are those who truly listen to their students' questions and find there authentic paths to explicit answers. A student willing to reveal ignorance is providing a treasure-trove of methodology for her teacher. We are powerful even in our ignorance. And you say to me, "All fine and dandy. But I am not a good person, not at all. Hatred comes easier to me than love. I resent almost everyone."

You forget. You aren't a story; you're an ongoing process. So am I. Right now, we are interfacing process-es; there may be something new in the outcome. Why are you speaking to me? Somewhere you have hidden some hope. Is it hope that you can find your way out to other people?

"That's too religious-sounding."

All right. Expectation. You possibly expect some-thing to come out of the process of this exchange with me. Just possibly, you *want* to discover a light out of your cave.

"Now, look, buddy boy. I don't want anything from you, and I don't need anything, and I'm not a cave person."

Why are you spending time with me?

"I—I, uh, don't know. I thought I'd better set you straight that there are folks who aren't going to dance to your slick take on how we tick."

Point taken. Lots of folks reject what I propose. But why do they—why do you—spend any energy at all on trying to evaluate it and then spend more energy rejecting it? Say it's all wrong. Crazy. Imagine everything you've been reading as one of those crazy graphic novels with ideas bouncing off walls and hair standing on end. Is there energy there, and if so, where does it come from? What energy makes you voice your objection to what I propose?

"What's crazy about those graphs? I have dozens of them."

Point! So, what's the energy that makes you read them? Why did you even pick up this book? And why are you engaging me right now? I'm asking if it isn't because, somewhere in your head's center, there is just a beginning curiosity about who I am, a response to my curiosity about who you are.

"Well, I don't know if I'm curious; I'd call it nosey."

Follow your nose and stick it into everything it finds. I maintain that's your innate desire to know.

"Know what?"

Anything and everything. You'll soon learn what's

really a waste of time and what's worth your time.

"How will I know?"

You will find yourself reaching for more of what's worthwhile, what's really expanding the best parts of you.

"You still think I have 'best parts.'"

Sure. You just spent how many minutes bringing out mine? Thank you.

"No problem."

Perhaps the most efficient guarantee that you can communicate with me is complete self-acceptance wherever in your personal process you find yourself. That means total acceptance—even ownership—of who you are at a given time. And for all the bad stuff that might haunt you and spark shame, never can you lose touch with the more intense flame of your goodness, beginning with your very existence. It means something, not in some big picture but in yourself, that you even exist. And with the acceptance of wherever you are in your individual processes, the more you will exist.

Writing such sentences is a risk, I know, because some reader might object that all the above is only "such stuff as dreams are made on." Oops, sorry. Shakespeare again (*The Tempest, 4.1.148*). Well, you don't have to be a Freud to recognize the value of dreams. They are clues to where you've come from and where it's possible for you to go. Langston Hughes counsels you to "Hold fast to dreams, for when dreams die, life is a broken-winged bird that cannot fly. Hold fast to dreams, for when dreams go, life is a barren field frozen with snow" (*Dreams*). Of course, such ideas seem rich as you ply your way through daily life's humdrum of familiar paths. But what's wrong with richness? Does the rehearsal of more hearty concepts than you're accustomed to cause you to aspire to growth? If so, reach, grab hold, and pull yourself to a new way of being. Just a bit. Hey, the next time I meet you may be inside a poem.

Just make sure the meter is dactylic. It's faster, and you have places to go.

5

EARTH

WHEN WE ARE children, our sense of the earth is blurred with our concept of the world, and it is usually defined by the parameters of our neighborhood and that of our closest grandparents. Television images of faraway places excite and perhaps confuse us about what is real, but eventually we have to own up to the fact that the earth is a pretty big hangout having little to do with our neighborhood or Grandpa's farm.

And then we find out that it has everything to do with our neighborhood in spite of what Grandpa might say.

"Mom, what's Thailand?" I ask as I look at the label of my shirt.

"Dad, why didn't you want to buy that new Accord?"

"Grandpa, why is our oat crop so tiny this year?"

"Nana, why do you only buy organic strawberries? Grandpa says that's nonsense."

You don't have to be a doctorate in something akin to macroeconomics to know that the answering of such questions can launch any number of courses in geography, global trade, agriculture, and climate change.

Most of us form our answers to those childhood questions on our own with help from TV newscasts and table conversations. Where we work, what courses in education we pursue, whether and where we invest, and myriad other associations are determined by how we answer those questions. And today, no matter what our answers are or what or how many degrees we have, we strongly sense that we ordinary individuals are vitally connected to the earth, wrong answers and all.

Some familiarity with history helps us, of course, and such a notion as "the New World" is a hefty clue as to how recently so-called Western civilization was clueless. After all, by 1492, the Italian Renaissance was already in its third century. And lest we too readily laugh at Columbus thinking he was already in India, how many of us moderns can fill in a blank map of Asia or the Middle East? With today's patterns of international trade and cultural exchanges, such ignorance becomes a blister, especially when it feeds overeager attempts to forestall immigration.

Nevertheless, all we know about the human race is on seven landmasses that probably emerged from the bodies of water surrounding them. These so-called continents and their 7.5 billion inhabitants form the surface of a not-so-giant globe (18.5 thousand miles in diameter) that is whirling on its axis at over eight hundred miles per hour, all the while pursuing an elliptical orbit around a giant sizzling star at a speed of seventy thousand miles per hour. Thanks to something called centrifugal force and the very gravity that frustrated our friend Einstein, everything and everybody stays in place. We haven't a clue we're moving at all, let alone in a double rotation in the middle of nowhere.

Ho-hum. How many times have we heard and/or read all that while remaining comfortably seated in our chair or at a desk, and how many times have we also forgotten all that because it doesn't affect us? But then, perhaps while working on Grandpa's farm, we spend time contemplating plain old dirt, perhaps rich soil. Then we remember a bit of anthropology and how our distant ancestors emerged from other species fed by the likes of that soil. It is then that we feel kin with the earth. Not even the Genesis parable dodged our relationship with dirt: Yahweh used clay to form Adam. We and the earth are one; we own each other.

Earth feeds and clothes us, bathes, warms, and cools us. It is not called "Mother" for nothing. But besides inheriting such a treasure, we have also inherited some very bad habits in our relationship with this grand provider. Only now are we becoming aware of the brink on which our Mother and we are perched.

Truth be told, Grandpa and Nana are on the same page with their oats and strawberries. The oat crop has dwindled because Grandpa has stopped using the amount of nitrogen-based fertilizers he was using until three years ago. Nana found out that with conventionally grown strawberries, she can't wash off the pesticides used to protect them or the fertilizer used in their plant soil. But Grandpa never read the article she read. Mom thinks it's a blessing for clothing laborers in Thailand to have work; Dad resents the resistance of Japan to marketing U.S.-made autos. Our family could be a seminar on the global village's thornier dimensions.

In fact, there now seems little time for seminars. There is enough scientific consensus to demand some immediate care about urgent life-and-death matters touching us and earth and earth's atmosphere. When, long ago, she supported the amazing species of dinosaurs, Mother Earth had no idea that man would one day mine their fossil remains for poison. Nor did she suspect that such poison could be heated and its lethal smoke pumped into the air. (Not even dinosaurs could breathe it.) And because such poisonous mining, burning, and pumping is an immense source of revenue, the entire process seems protected, even privileged enough to escape effective controls.

It isn't long before daydreaming about such nightmares renders them quite personal, as in "How am I connected to these issues, and what can I do about them?"

First off, we face an irony in that our first doing might well be "not doing." We participate in so many networks via our consumerism. Where we have choices, we must begin to discover how the earth's predicament is affected by them. We love animals, and we love our desserts. How are they connected? Our favorite sorbet is made with palm oil. Our favorite great ape is the orangutan, both Bornean and Sumatran. And? The orangutan is the ape most threatened with a loss of habitat extinction because of palm oil plantations. Another type of sorbet, please.

More extensively, all of us need to educate ourselves with the industries behind our food supplies. We must realize how one crop or product might affect another. A starting place just might be in the library with such near-classics as Michael Pollan's *The Omnivore's Dilemma*. Not to worry, Michael's not a vegetarian. Books and articles lead to other books and articles. Before long, it is relatively simple to realize a prioritized catalog: "needed/not so needed," and "harmful/not so harmful," which begins to govern our shopping lists and even dares to accompany us to stores. We become alarmed at how much we don't need or even want.

As often happens when our behavior changes, our topics of conversation change as well as our energy and frequency with those topics. We share what we have discovered. We have not only put the palm oil back on the shelf, but we've also become active educators among our peers. Some of them don't even read lists of ingredients or tables of nutritional facts on food labels. Behold. A curriculum for the most recent teachers of earth's folks: first, labels; then, social agronomy or something. Pity our new friend-students if they visit the zoo with us.

But then, we have to get to the zoo. Two methods: bus or private car/cab. Two types of bus: both diesel, one minimal exhaust. Two types of car: one electric with no exhaust. A new guest to the conversation: compromise. The lesser of two evils. Yes, climate change due to fossil fuel emissions has proven itself an evil threat to existence as we earthlings know it. Unless we know the electric car is recharging on renewable energy (e.g., wind or sun panel), our choice must be the bus with less exhaust and more wasted time getting to the orangutan exhibit.

But on the way, what an education on primate nutrition awaits us. For about half of its downtown stops, passengers are likely to be "two-and-a-halves," your nickname for large folks who take up, well, two seats anyway. Often enough, they are in motorized wheelchairs. After a few minutes and a few stops along the way after they board, such folks are quite likely to dig into their carry-on bags, looking for something to eat. Invariably, the choice is an always-ready bag of chips, that ever-ready boon to their diet and to the cause for healthy nutrition. Hence their weight and size when more is only better for cane makers and clothiers. How about a piece of fruit?

Next stop, the great apes displays. Sure enough, fresh vegetables—yes, Oliver, kale and spinach—all over the place and lots of attentive munching. How much to learn at the zoo. Nationally and even internationally, zoological gardens have become much less entertaining than brave efforts to save species. In fact, there is plenty of evidence that more intelligent sensitivity cares for the preservation of wild animals than for the human habitat.

The bottom line is that the bottom has to move up as our list of what we need shortens. We simply must make do with less. We must use less of the earth's resources, never mind how clever we've been as a race that could invent its way out of so many needs. Are they really needs? Or are they just *wants*, stuff we've grown accustomed to having at our disposal? Electric lights when daylight through windows is more than enough? Running water through every step in brushing the teeth, shaving, or washing dishes? Hot water when cold will do the trick equally well? Refrigerator doors standing open while we get out everything we need for that salad? And then that combustible engine issue.

Do we really need to be operating two cars simultaneously, each transporting just one person? Can a drop-off be planned or a bus used to free one car. Do we really even need to own two cars or more? And do we stay on schedule with maintenance of the one car we must have so that the engine operates efficiently? And must we fly, or do we have time to take a train or a bus to the West Coast? Oh, and this book. Is it just sentimentality that makes us prefer paper over an electronic screen? And did the author bother to ensure the publisher used recycled paper? Oopsie. More endangered habitat.

Before big finance found the treasures in children's toys, we played in the dirt with homemade cars and trucks, snitched spoons for shovels, and, with the help of some water and mud, managed some fine sculptures. Dirt. How we took it for granted. Now it might be a rich support to a meditation on just what it is and what it took to get where it is: at the bottom of things.

Except that it's really at the top of things, isn't it? The very surface of Mother Earth. What is it, what does it mean, where does it lead my dreams? Dirt. How varied, how malleable, how mysterious. Yes, we came from that after we got out of the water, that other part of Mother Earth's very surface. So fluid, so beautiful, so treacherous, such salt, such life. And do we have time to just sit and wonder about it? Is our lack of careful responsibility a sign of our lack of meditation, daydreaming, wondering? Do we need more recess time?

Such nagging. The points were made long ago and just dismissed or forgotten. Enough, already. We've got gardening to do. Do you really need that large a container of Roundup? Cutting back must become the name of our game. Easier is not going to be better anymore. Perhaps muscle must replace chemicals in the garden. Saving time will not be as important as helping save the environment.

But our environment is changing, you remind us all. Some think it cannot endure as a safe haven for us till the end of this millennium. Just how much can we contribute to offset the mighty and myriad eruptions of imbalance and corrosion of earth and its atmosphere? You hate to sound defeatist, but why should you bother since our world will not exist in 3000? But wait! Maybe you can help slow the destructive forces down a bit. Maybe ensure a supportive atmosphere for your great-great-grandkids to breathe. Maybe you can get aligned with more human help than you realize is around if you increase your teaching skills about these matters. Maybe.

It could be that mankind will have to treat the earth as it has treated so much else in the consumptive plague that is waste: use it and discard it. Throw the wrapper on the ground, or into space. It could be that it's time to move on. Where? Hey, it's a big universe out there. Scientists and astronauts have been exploring it for decades, always looking for another atmosphere that will accommodate us and that we will—er, uh—*preserve*! Yes, that's the word.

But that's such a risky adventure, invoking both life and death.

What was the discovery of our third world countries on hitherto unknown continents? Very dangerous but very necessary. Was it a piece of cake for a Welsh widow to migrate to Bangkok as a tutor for royal children? Perhaps our own migrations could be as graceful as Anna Loenowens's. Who knows but that there may be brand-new music we could make as beautiful as Anna's and Mongkut's, the king of Siam. "Shall We Dance?" will have to wait on "Shall We *Chance* It?"

For all that, it may well be that we indeed cannot rescue our environment or ourselves. We may have to move and once again do what we can be good at, imagine and invent. But precisely where would we go and how, and how many of us will be able to make the transition? Had we been at these questions fifty years ago, we would have had to include accommodation for a specialized wheelchair in the first vehicle out. Stephen Hawking, who predicted the end of this world just two weeks before he died, was acutely scientific, clear-sighted, and human. Might he have been a new Columbus, only better at reading maps? He would have calmed Albert Einstein's frustration at seeing the expansion of the universe after he had convinced himself it should be shrinking. But Stephen would eventually have respected Einstein's splendid humanity. Indeed, sublime humanity, humility, and care will have to be the hallmarks of such a new launch.

Hallmarks, indeed. And cannot humanity, humility, and care guide all of us right now as we mightily try to prevent the Grand Matricide? Perhaps the very first effort must be to realize the choices bearing on our environment's welfare, choices that confront us every footstep or channel change. Awareness of the best responses to such choices is our preparation for inhabiting new territory wherever we may find it.

Is it too difficult for someone who doesn't know what states border Pennsylvania to begin exploring the greater universe, looking for a home? All the really tough groundwork has been done by our scientists. But do we even follow such groundwork at all? Do we even know the current status of the International Space Station and what it is investigating? Do we care? If we don't, then perhaps the whereabouts and status of the Hubble Space Telescope can only be a post-graduate course for us. After all, we might ask, how many Spaniards were interested in coming to Latin America in 1500? And before 1849, how many Americans would have been interested in the West Coast. Except for gold. Might there be gold on Mars? Is that what it takes? Could it be that the god of war, Mars, has seen enough of the cat-fights over religion on earth? He just might be luring us away from our planet before we completely destroy it in the name of other gods.

It is time for science non-fiction to replace its less careful cousin on our nightstands and reading lists. We can handle it. The key might be in a vivid realization that most of these experiments involve human beings making huge sacrifices to explore space possibilities, some without even leaving our planet. Someday we might be asked to live a completely different lifestyle. Perhaps it is time to become realistically interested in such a possibility.

Can we love Mother Earth enough to leave her?

6

HUMOR

THE OLD TRICK. Ha! Earth weighs 5.972×10^{24} kilograms. Heavy chapter followed with something light and funny. Except that discussing humor can be anything but light and funny. "Humor me" might be a command to "Read my humors" in the Greek sense of the four basic humors. Usually, of course, it means "Tell me a joke; make me laugh."

How complicated it all gets. After all, isn't a human to be dignified and serious, not crumpled over in dangerous ("I thought I'd split a gut!") hysteria?

Yet how important laughter is precisely because it undermines so much posturing and pretense. First of all, it requires some courage. "She doesn't appreciate humor," "Oh no, not another joke," or "Here comes the clown; cheer us up, clown!" Introductions like that are lethal. "Make me laugh" kills any chance for quick and easy humor. "Oh, I'd love to, but I forgot my mirror" might just work. The reflex that finds such a response quickly is called wit. But wit is more than a sense of humor; it is intelligent consciousness first. It is wit, though, that makes humor possible: the capacity to see more than one side of any situation, more than one side of any group of words.

So often, wit and humor are identified with language and key words. A useful distinction might be that comedians tell jokes, while comics just tell things funnily. A comic is an actor who can immediately define his relationship to a situation without depending on language. A sudden sag of the shoulders and drastic relaxation of facial muscles can indicate weakness, confusion, or fear. A definite turn of the head to focus on the person or object that is the source of the threat or challenge just might bring the house down if the introduction and invitation to entertain were explicit. Yes, it's very complicated, but a good clown can summon up such mechanisms and fill them with believable emotion.

Everyone knows that a crucial part of getting a— TIMING. And of course, that's the—TIMING. Oh well, you get the joke. Nobody can define *timing*, but the best delivery allows the audience to get to the punch just a nanosecond before the comic delivers it. In that scenario, the audience owns the joke. Sometimes timing has to do with just taking up time with silence. But silence must have a reason and/or motivation in even the most casual of performances. Quite often, it gives the listeners time to imagine the situation. They can get left behind in a complex or rushed delivery of the details that make the joke work. Often the comic can help with just a key silent action illustrating a character in the narrative. Perhaps the most effective orchestrator of such silence was the comic Jack Benny. His trademark slow turn of the head with a slight smile on his lips and his eyes surveying all of space, searching for an explanation of what he'd just heard was golden humor. And so often, the joke was on him.

Humility is an almost automatic trigger for laughter when the situation is formal performance. The stage or other performance space just about enshrines the performer as, well, hot stuff. Great. Worthy of our focused laughter and applause. So, when the center of all this attention contradicts such a setup, it's funny. The most common choices in so many comic situations were pants falling down, a pie in the face, and slipping on a banana peel.

But why? Why do such things make us laugh? What is the essential trigger that sets off a situation as comic?

First of all, the setting has to allow it, and a formal "pay on the way in" performance is far from being

The author being incongruous.

the only environment facilitating humor. An early-morning coffee klatch among old friends exists precisely because the atmosphere is one in which anything can happen or be said. And a well-placed (timed) and haughty "Well!" can be quite funny after someone's too candid remark. Eye-rolls can serve the same purpose. Indeed, facial features and their maneuvers have outrun the need for clown makeup in today's circus formats. When audiences watched a solitary clown, for example, the late, great Lou Jacobs, perform with his little dog, spectators and clown were easily more than a block away from each other in such venues as Madison Square Garden or a five-ring tent. Such distances made emphasizing the smiling mouth and raised eyebrows with greasepaint necessary. With the American adoption of one-ring tents, faces do very well without makeup. The audiences can read natural, unpainted faces reacting with exaggerated expressions.

But what is the germ? What is the general ingredient in any comic situation that sparks laughter? For too long, it was presumed that a juxtaposition of incongruities bred comedy. An overdressed gentleman (think top hat and a monocle) walking across the stage slips on a banana peel and falls down. Laughter if the character feels only indignity, since he is above such an event. But if he writhes in pain and is unable to stand? At best, there is only confusion over whether that was supposed to happen. It's not funny anymore. But a juxtaposition of incongruities is still maintained.

Similarly, the pie in the face mechanism. Whipped cream (or is it Rapid Shave, which is cheaper?) everywhere, especially the face. The audience is shocked when the pie comes out of nowhere and silences the haughty mouth. The clown runs off, and the other clowns carry on with the sketch, with everything in order through the next three acts. But then comes the ambulance siren, the paramedics running backstage, and clumsiness and incongruities juxtaposed everywhere. No laughter now. The foam has suffocated the clown. Not funny!

In both cases, accidents have derailed the characterization. The incongruities blur when the character must stop playing the haughty role and become a distressed human being. "Playing a role" is the key. Comedy is always theater in some measure. Even a parlor invitation to "Make us laugh" addressed to a particular individual evokes that person's informal reputation as the group's clown and grants him humble theatrical license.

A grand portion of our interest in humor is driven by a need to explain that bizarre, near-spasmodic reaction: laughter. So, analysis into what laughter is and precisely what causes it seems hand in hand with humor and less dramatic happiness.

There are gradations of laughter, near parallels to the gradations of happiness. Laughter is more obvious, more physically expressed, just a sometimes occasion of happiness. Laughter is often too sudden a reaction for an individual to take stock of his degree of happiness. He just laughs, and then, from the outside in, happiness can be evoked. The fact that psychological science has, for years, studied the mechanism of laughter indicates how intricate a process it might be. And even without a thoroughly satisfactory analysis of laughter, it has become a staple of several protocols of therapy.

What happens in the phenomenon we call laughter?

"I totally lost it. He is so funny!"

Certainly, there is some measure of control loss.

Helplessness reigns for a few moments as we crow the unmistakable voiced exhalations we call laughter. In extreme instances, we may have to hold onto something to steady ourselves, and we may even double up or bend over, pointing to the person or situation that makes us laugh. But there is more. Just hearing ourselves, hearing our own laughter, seems to reset the trigger that set us off in the first place.

Whatever is or isn't going on in the brain at such moments certainly takes its cue from surprise. "You can't see it coming!" is a deft compliment about punch lines and comic movements. We are caught off the guard of composure. Neuron traffic aligning along one narrative track suddenly encounters a synaptic traffic jam and must re-route. When the five-and-a-half times Lane Bryant lady is sent into the "Laser Reducer" cabinet, the crank is turned, and a loud bang springs the door open to release a midget dressed as the lady, the laughter is guaranteed. Yet the laughter is really on us for *not* seeing it coming. There is perfect logic in such humor. Punch lines in verbal humor and the so-called "blow-off" in visual gags must exhibit logic of some dimension, usually exaggerated. Well, what did you expect?

In such cases, we have put ourselves in a situation where we expect to laugh, maybe even in the extreme—"I have to tell you the best joke I've heard in weeks"—or a trip to the circus or a comedy nightclub is a prologue to laughter. In both situations, permission is granted for laughter. In the first, the narrator may be smiling from his opening, "Two guys go out to dinner," all the way through the punchline, when he laughs outright and we join him with open-throated laughter. In the second and third situation, even the cotton candy or cocktails are laughing.

In the act of laughing itself, we change. There is a degree of control-loss, often expressed in the extreme—"I thought I'd wet my pants!"—and frequently, focus on the person or scene provoking the laugh is surrendered. We are just laughing to hear ourselves laughing, as it were. But that hearing of our own laughter can sustain or rekindle the heat of the original burst, and the laugh recurs. Besides, it feels good.

Enhancing your intake of oxygen, laughter energizes your heart and breathing and increases the release of peptides within your brain, producing an opiate effect. It can stimulate the production of natural painkillers and strengthen the immune system. It's fun. And because the sound of our own laughter is so suggestive, we very often attribute the intensity and length of a laugh to our ability to hear others laughing along with us. For this reason, prolonged and extreme laughing is often defined as a social phenomenon. We laugh most with other laughers.

But it is very definitely possible to start yourself laughing without any provocation at all except your desire to laugh. It is possible to sustain solitary laughter that is so genuine the sound alone provokes laughter in others. Ask any actor. Actors are called to laugh "out of the blue" quite often. In fact, one acting coach demonstrating this and provoking his students with curious grins, giggles, and guffaws began rolling on the floor, roaring his amusement, and then he accidentally lost his breath, began coughing and gasping. The students thought it was part of the demonstration and laughed all the more. Recovering and standing up, the instructor explained to them what had happened, and they were embarrassed.

The sound of laughter itself is funny and contagious. Right now, writing or reading these words, a person can just release the first monosyllable of a chuckle that will likely set off a very illogical but polysyllabic set of voiced breaths that are so infectious that there develops an outright laugh replicating itself until the neighbors or pets are disturbed and the decision is made to stop—hopefully, with breathing unscathed. The trick that actors employ depends on the memory of the laughing sound itself as funny. And that sound reproduced is, in turn, laughed at until a chain reaction is set up. Try it. Of course, you'll sound ridiculous, but that's the idea.

On a bright, sunny morning last week, a very large man stepped onto the bus and greeted all the passengers in a deep, booming voice before paying his fare. Then he disparaged the lack of response to his greeting and, with a large, deep intonation of "Oh, I know!" set off on a lone laughing binge as he made his way to the rear of the coach. If he stopped, it was to bellow the day's weather forecast in between guffaws, and then, with an insult to the forecasters, he soared into thundering solo laughter again. After a few minutes of this, there were smiling faces and stifled giggles throughout the bus. Why *stifled*? From his entrance onto the bus, a judgment had been made that "Oh, another nut case is joining us." And there is an uncomfortable consensus that one shouldn't laugh at the mentally disturbed. Express analyses of such a person would chalk such behavior up to an anti-social syndrome and abnormal compulsive behavior. But one wonders whether he was normal enough to be laughing at himself, as he walked through three inches of snow two days later.

Although it requires a distinct act of the will to start, once those first and second "syllables" of laughter are made and heard, the follow-through and gradual amplification become easier and more automatic. Sometimes a lone laugher in his apartment can be laughing for five minutes or so. At the close of such an episode, the person may feel exhausted, depending on the amount of energy expended, but invariably, he or she feels better than before the laugh. Here, again, the brain releases endorphin peptides that soothe.

A fundamental example of laughter's social dimension can be found in the behavior of a four-year-old gorilla at the Milwaukee Zoo. Suleiman has more than ninety-seven-percent of our DNA. Walking upright, he will quicken his steps and then dive into a series of somersaults on the floor of his display, only to pick up a blanket and pull it over his entire body as he comes out of the last full-body rotation. The clincher comes when he slowly peeks out from under the blanket and checks the audience. For laughter? After all, he does this maneuver a dozen times a day.

There is scientific evidence that laughter is not only a reaction but, under some circumstances, a chosen action instigating a positive feeling and increased motivation to encounter the workaday tasks a person must face. Often after such a moment has been enjoyed, we hear, "Ya gotta laugh!" in recognition of the near-therapeutic quality of such an experience. The laughter could have begun in the company of another who is also enjoying the moment, but there is a moment of decision when one or both parties can accept and even prolong the laughing because it seems almost an analgesic. Indeed, the popularity of laugh-therapy studios has increased alongside those that teach yoga and meditation.

It could be that the bravest moment in the composition of Western literature is the gravedigger scene in Shakespeare's *Hamlet*. Unjustly accused of murder, cleverly escaping a foreign execution, barely returned to his homeland incognito, Hamlet finds his best friend, Horatio, and they go for a walk that takes them through a cemetery. Lo, they happen upon a grave being prepared by a drunken gravedigger, who is sharp enough to trade jests and sing his favorite ditty, "A Pickaxe and a Spade." Typically, we know more than the characters on the stage seem to, and we can sense the grave is being prepared for Ophelia, Hamlet's girlfriend. So, we have been set up to view the momentous grief with which Hamlet will find out his love is dead. Then the digger throws up a skull that just happens to be that of Hamlet's birthday clown, Yorick, the king's jester. There is perhaps no other scene so loaded with emotion for both the audience and Hamlet, and Hamlet himself is invited to consider humor. We wait. Alas, poor Hamlet.

And how about that king's jester position, so common throughout England and parts of Europe? What is the reasoning behind such a custom, and do we incorporate such a character in today's halls of power?

Given the amount of authority and control weighted in one individual, a monarch, there seems to have been a recognition that alternative visions, including comic ones and grotesque ones, be presented. Since there were risky negative dimensions in such visions, humor was an important ambiance in delivering any message to a king. So, even though some deliveries had to be negative and critical of the throne, *jester* was the title and overall function of such an often dangerous position. But it should not be missed that the court jester, fool, or clown was preeminently employed, lest anyone take themselves too seriously.

In the centers of political power today, even the committees and special commissions take themselves too seriously so that, effectively, they do not always provide the balance of opinion that decision-makers may need. But in today's media, so rapidly expansive and technological, there seems to be the capacity for something like the jesting of old. At first, the term "pundit" seemed rude and misplaced for those in the various branches of the press corps. Too often, the term is directly related to the currently devalued "pun," which, to the modern ear, indicates a remark just north of a play on words. When one realizes, first, that it takes background and knowledge to turn a pun, and second, that "pundit" is directly related to the Hindu "pandita," a learned man, calling experienced newscasters and columnists pundits seems fitting. Not even some jesters got the frequency of laughter that some contemporary pundits enjoy. But the likeness to "jester" is now appreciated, and every once in a while, the message does hinge on a pun. Freedom of the media is now greatly valued as we surf from Fox News to CNN and the PBS News Hour in search of sound policymaking.

By "comic relief," a reference is made to the use of lightheartedness and laughter for relaxation in an otherwise formal and tenser situation. On the one hand, such comedy is not terribly difficult to effect since the situation just about begs for it; on the other, it takes great courage to outrightly inject it into a rather stiff and serious setting.

The function of the typical funereal eulogy is often seen as a place to not only honor the deceased but to celebrate her as well. This is often achieved via quotations, often very humorous ones, from the lighter moments in the dead person's life. Some eulogists even allow themselves the repetition of a joke once played on the deceased person. The effect is always a lightening of the atmosphere of the setting.

"Daddy called a man who turned in front of him an asshole while we were driving into the church parking lot!"

"Nana farted the whole way to mass last Sunday!"

Religion and religious situations almost call for jest. The outward intensity of such ceremony is almost at odds with the everyday routines that assemble the

modern congregation. It only takes a slight impropri-
ety in the sanctuary to set off more than a ripple of
giggles—juxtaposition of incongruities, indeed. Such
are attacks of giggles on the part of an altar server or
two, bells rung at the wrong times, or tripping on the
strange lengths of those cassocks.

But is it really possible to have an incongruity in
such scenarios? Might a joke in the sanctuary instead
be seen as most congruous? If any participant or pre-
sider in such a ceremonial time were asked what the
occasion for the ritual was, the answer would finally get
around to a chance for humanity to honor and praise
its roots, its creator, or its savior. "Hey, God! This is
who we are, and you know it better than we do." If we
are truly celebrating a Creator and Creation, the entire
work is up for ceremonial grace and blessing.

Once, during the seventies, at the main Sunday
celebration in the Cathedral of St. Francis de Sales in
Oakland, California, a crawling infant sitting near the
front scrambled up into the sanctuary. The congregation managed a wave of laughter, and the priest cel-
ebrant, completely unruffled, picked the baby up and,
holding him aloft, made the sign of the cross with him
over the assembled faithful. More laughter, but en-
riched and sacred. Not a bit of incongruity anywhere.

Children enjoy a special place in any discussion
of humor. From the time they discover the magic in

"Peek-a-boo," they sense they can control at least part of the world around them. Once their hands go in front of their eyes, the world disappears, and they disappear to the world. This simple little game translates with growth into all sorts of innocent projections that are rich occasions of humor. Because the game is theirs, when an adult does it, they immediately recognize it as humorous. Even if it does still hold some magic and power, it is a funny thing to believe.

Youth and inexperience lend themselves to a kind of innocence that makes possible the simplest funny games. Teasing competitions are a case in point. "Oh, can't I have this shoe?" Quite often, unless fear prevails, if the child recognizes the impossible size differences or the stupidity of having only one shoe, a puzzled smile is the minimal reward. Holding the speaker's foot next to the much smaller one is a literal juxtaposition of incongruities.

These days, supermarkets seem rigged for comedy with kids. The shopping carts made to look like police squad vehicles just cry out for a kooky expression on an adult face and the question, "Officer, are you keeping the speed limit?" Rides in the shopping carts of any shape suggest the advice, "I hope you're paying the taxi driver a big tip!" And if the shopping cart is already full of merchandise, the parent or eye contact cannot be stressed enough.

For any such monkeyshines, eye contact is paramount, first with the child and then a quick glance to the parents. They will give the first review of what will be a split-second act in the treasured long drama too often taken for granted as childhood amusement. Both the eyes and the overall face should be smiling to indicate harmlessness. Often, that's automatic just because of the charm children are lucky enough to wear in the first place. And if the kid is already smiling, a bit of humor seems a cinch. "Oh, I'm glad I got here early, because you're going to get all the good stuff." Sometimes the parents can get into the scene. Once, referencing the child in the cart with "Oh, where did you find those? Are they expensive? Are they on sale?" prodded the young father to quip, "No, these, you have to make yourself!" with the mother adding, "And they're very expensive!"

Kids seem to be meant for playing games, and they know it. And truth be told, there are few larger games than grocery shopping with Mom. Even if the adventure doesn't include a ride in the rolling basket, there's the promise of eating events galore and guessing what she might be persuaded to buy. And then there's all that interaction with other kids, larger families, different races. It's a holiday. So, when an adult joins in with something like "Oh, that's the one I wanted!" with smiling eye contact, almost always, there's smiles and laughs all around. And the most fun? Meeting up with a rolling basket that has two little tots riding in it along with the groceries. Eye contact. Smile of anticipation on the adult and "Oh, can I ride, too?"

This chapter must end with a text message just in from Albert Einstein:

Equation on earth's mass might mean more to U.S. readers if it's in tons. What the hell is a kilogram to modern Americans? Guys at Princeton even had trouble with it at first: 5.792×10^{21} TONS.

7

INFINITY

LITERALLY *NO END* or *no border.* Applicable to time and space, both concepts are heavily dependent on fairly intricate mental juggling. Is it even imaginable? Has it been experienced? Just what does that lazy eight or *to the nth* signify? What does it mean to say that infinity even exists? Has anyone been there and back? If it is no exact thing, condition, or experience, can it be anything? If it is nothing, does it contradict every statement about it? Does it have to exist?

Probably the most active discussions of infinity occur in religious contexts standing for whatever the next phase of human existence is. In such contexts, the vagueness of its referent is ignored and what is left of a concept is used with the rigor of certitude. But eternal beings and their connections with life on earth get a bit of a clip and definition with the formula ending so many prayers: "forever and ever. Amen." Of course, *ever* is recognized as infinity, but *amen*, while a voiced agreement to whatever precedes it, most often signifies no more than the definite ending of a prayer. "Forever and ever. Amen" can almost be considered a contradiction. Is it possible that infinity and its relation, eternity, could be impossible to limit within the letters of a word? In the triumphant roar of religious invocations, does not the brain detect Macbeth's "sound and fury...signifying nothing" (Shakespeare, *Macbeth*, 5.5.27–28)?

It is literally impossible to define *infinity* since the definition of its nature imposes limits and borders. It seems impossible as well to imagine *infinity* since the closest experience we have with it is measured time and distance. Such questions raise a key challenge to infinity itself: whether it exists at all apart from mathematical theory that, through lack of definition, will never be complete.

8

MEASUREMENT

THE MOMENT EINSTEIN won't share with us, of course, is when he coaxed our planet to step up on the scale in the first place. And just how much would such a scale weigh?

Anyone with even a high school physics course tucked away in their academic baggage can figure it out pretty well. Something like multiplying a unit or section of earth-mass by the size of the earth, which can be calculated from the circumference.

More fun would be calculating the source of a speedometer that got Einstein and his pals the speed of light.

Everything is measurement, so we're left wondering just what measurement is. No matter what is being measured, size, weight, or velocity, solid or liquid, particle or wave, measurement seems to depend on some manner of comparison. Get something you want to use as a standard, maybe a straight stick. (Slow down; it isn't a yardstick yet!) How many times can you place that stick down along your backyard's perimeter? Voila, you just found out the length and width of your new lawn. What if you can only place it twenty times across the northern edge and there is still some that won't require the entire length of the stick? Oh! The stick will have to be calibrated into equal sections so that we can report twenty and a fourth sticks. And maybe because we are assessing the size of a yard, could the old stick just be called a yardstick? By the time you happen to notice your bare foot takes up only a third of the stick, you're on your way to discovering a foot-long ruler (or Subway sandwich).

Comparison to that measured stick will yield both area and volume of a solid. But what of liquids? What are they compared to? How much rain has fallen on my new lawn? Easy. An Irishman grabs a bucket and sets it inside a measured area of the lawn. After the storm, he checks how full the bucket is. It just so happens that the Celtic word for *pail* passes through medieval Latin, Anglo-Norman French, and Middle English as something like *gallon*. And *quart*? Well, you remember your bare foot.

Certainly, that pail and that stick will have to be

taken care of so that everyone's sticks and pails will have some standard to compare them with. You can do what the folks of the National Bureau of Standards are doing: get yourself a vacuum and then measure how far light travels during 1/299,792,458 of a second. (Oh, but that's a meter stick. A yardstick would be just a little less: 0.9144 of the meter.)

And so on with the strength of light, the volume of sound, and their effect on more and more sophisticated instruments. No matter what the dials and black boxes look like, though, they are just comparing an amount of light or sound to a once arbitrary standard.

And so it goes till we encounter motion and time. One exists—kinda—and the other doesn't. Really. Look out the front window and observe someone walking on their way to work. They are certainly not at rest. They are moving. How fast? And you've stumbled on the need for the invention of time: a measurement of motion. That's all it is. Get out the yardstick and measure a length of the sidewalk. Maybe put a couple of marks down: the one the man will cross first and the one he will cross at the end of your experiment. Forget all the clocks in the house and on your phone or wrist. Just (ahem) watch. The duration between his crossing the first and second marks (fifteen steps or "I recited the Lord's Prayer twice!") is called time. Does it exist? Is there any such "thing" as *time*?

Not apart from that man's walking. There is no time in the sense that there is that stick and maybe those measurements of your yard or detections of a flashlight inside your vacuum.

Wait a minute! I will quit writing (oh, please!) in fifty-four minutes. What are those minutes, if not time? The minutes are the calibration of an hour, or one twenty-fourth of the duration of the earth's rotation toward and then away from the sun. Again, it's an arbitrary measurement of motion. Minute's up! Keep writing. Ha! How do you know the minute's up? You looked at the digital register on your phone. Where's the motion in that? I suppose there's a central computer with a moving hard drive that dispatches phone apps, dates, and times. Pretty much.

And frighteningly, if there is no such thing as time, there is no yesterday, tomorrow, or this afternoon. There is only *now*. *Then* and *not yet* are figments of the imagination and language. Such concepts should not be devalued, however. Cherished memories and persistent hope enrich our experience of *now*. They are components of who we are. But they only exist in our memories and imaginations. That's not to say they don't greatly enrich our experience of the present. As such, they are what allows our minds to give importance to recess times.

What about God and infinity and all that? Whoever

and whatever God might be, it doesn't do recess. God is just *is*. Maintenance of all the *is-ing* that is is all there is for the source of all being. Everything is present. And without memory or imagination, recess has no meaning. Infinity, too, is simply an intensely *is-ing* present. There simply (confusing as it may be) is no time. There is only *is*.

To err is human, but it feels divine. Besides the humor in the line, there is a bit of theological wisdom. Whoever and whatever God is and regardless of one's religion or lack thereof, it is the source and continuous support of all being. That more than suggests that for us to be is for us to participate in whatever that source is called. So, to be human is also to be divine regardless of what we label "erroneous" or how much we reject religion.

Learning how to measure everything that makes up our physical universe was the propaedeutic to science, that generic word for knowledge that has become oh-so specialized over and over. Science is little else besides the relationships between measurements. From distance to dentistry, radiation to refraction, and bacteriology to botany, there is heavy dependence on measurements. And to facilitate comparisons between relationships, the metric system was introduced in France and quickly adopted by science as the standard language for units of measurement. (After all, foot sizes differ.)

Baha'i measurment, Delhi, India

Inca measurement, Ollantaytambo, Peru

It isn't too far a stretch to find poetry in science, or for that matter, theology. If, in measurement, everything is relatable, then at least an analogous unity should be perceptible in an apparently heterogeneous universe. Dentistry does search and command distances; for radiation to be accurate, there must be heavy dependence on refraction, and for botany to succeed, it must be apprised of the state of incumbent bacteriology. For that matter, indicator lights from radiography are blinking in the dentist's office. And don't forget the doctor's specially designed and illuminated refractor for better vision in the mouth or the routine inspection tracking the use of antibacterial lotions and gloves in and around the chair area. And on and on.

So, where's that poetry? It is not so much the poetry of language but of things. After all, the poetry of language comprises words appropriating the relationships of things. Juliet's "A rose by any other name would smell as sweet" might be scientifically countered with "Yes, but the name *rose* is just a cognate for something richly colored and scented; it is almost a measurement." For all her loving romance, she waxes rather scientific on her balcony by reminding us of the unit of measurement for sweet smells. Gertrude Stein's poetry was just more persistent in her "A rose is a rose is a rose" four hundred years later. But while substances technically referred to by very specific terminology are often related in equations by letters, their relationships can be seen as carrying an almost emotional force that is poetic. Thus, the relationship between force, mass, and acceleration is poetic because they are related and interdependent in $F = MA$.

And the theology? The being or existence that is a fundamental driver and source of all that stuff mathematically related through measurement? Isn't that universal relationship whatever we're trying to identify as God—if the definition is not too religious or cultic.

And just as we're about to count the old bartenders and chefs as the original scientists because of their preoccupations with measurement, Julia Child comes up with "Oh, put lots of butter in. That's what makes it good!" or "Now you can put fruit juice in this dessert, but it's my birthday, so I'm going to put in all the alcohol I can!" Nevertheless, even in the proportions observed by the most freewheeling of our cooks and mixologists, we find instinctive measurement. Habit has long since rendered a quarter of a teaspoon as a "pinch" and two tablespoons as a "splash."

Measurements and the numerals and alphabets that allow us to record them have enabled comparisons throughout existence. A visit to the zoo presents too familiar comparisons in the primate and ape displays. But the attempt of a young giraffe to kiss a human spectator yields some bizarre comparisons. First of all, the animal has to get its head and stubby horns through the cable fence barrier. That takes some not-so-graceful cooperation between those long front legs and that wonder of nature (and science), the neck. Finally, the long black tongue right in front of the spectator's face erases all the fascination and charm in a fraction of a second. Then there is the long process of the head backing through the fence and the legs righting themselves just as the spectator notices a nearby placard stating that the necks of mice, humans, and giraffes all have the same number of vertebrae. Reenter fascination and charm (neck and neck with poetry?) thanks to science and measurement.

If measurement could be seen as a unifier of all that is, its effects would have to be discernible not only in science but in art. It might even be seen as an avenue to relating the different art forms: painting, sculpture, music, literature, film, dance, and drama. That's admittedly a lot to relate, but it's nothing compared to the entire material universe! A cinch.

The decision to make a painting begins with the measurement of canvas, wood, glass, or other material onto which the paint will be applied. Early on, the artist's efforts are literally "framed." Inside of such a parameter, either nature dictates proportions between elements of figuration or it is rejected outrightly, as is the case in much modern and postmodern work. Especially if the artist is using natural forms to realize her imagination, those forms must relate to each other as they relate in nature so that the spectator can recognize what they represent. The proportions of trees, houses, horizons, and human figures must be calculated after those in nature. That requires measurement. Even deliberate distortions of nature such as the notable elongations of El Greco demand proportional respect so that an arm can still be recognizable as an arm in comparison with the rest of a human figure.

Aside from photographic or realistic painting, unrecognizable objects are given arbitrary relationships within the boundaries of a given modern work, but those relationships are actually proportions that are measured. The soft-edged unequal rectangles so common to Mark Rothko works demand measurable decisions on which rectangle will be larger, where the blurring should begin between the panels, and how wide the irregular painted frame should be in which the panels "float."

One of the most famous sculptures in the world appears to be a very realistic portrayal of a nude young man. But Michelangelo's *David*, nicknamed "il Gigante," is seventeen feet tall. The realism is in very measured proportions relating shoulder width to arm length and arm length to thigh placement of the left hand. The efforts to calibrate carefully might have been severely multiplied since the original block of Carrara marble Buonarotti worked on had been laid out already for a sitting and clothed portrayal of the same prophet. So, the very top of David's head was at the very edge of that block of marble.

The use of chapters, stanzas, acts, and scenes in written art are in themselves measured units organizing the treatment of subject matter, character development, and plotted movement for a narrative line. While the measurement here is strictly imagined, it must still remain proportionate. For instance, the outline for this book includes this and the following chapter as treating "measurement" and "art" respectively. But the calculated or measured topics discussed in this chapter must treat measurement in art without anything approximating a discussion of the nature of art itself. In the case of poetry, of course, much of the power retained by distilled language results from the calibrated measurement of meter, an *iambic foot* being the most common in English: /u -/. Yet stanzas and other units are themselves demarcated by how much of the theme is developed in each. A Shakespearian sonnet, for instance, is fourteen lines of iambic pentameter with the rhyme scheme changing every four lines until the last couplet, which rhymes. On top of all that, there is a problem expressed in the first eight lines, solved in the last six. Rhyme schemes are counted repetitions of the same sound stressing an image or idea and are codified by letters of the alphabet. Thus, Shakespeare's Sonnet 29:

When in disgrace with fortune and men's eyes,	A
I all alone beweep my outcast state,	B
And trouble deaf heaven with my bootless cries,	A
And look upon myself and curse my fate,	B
Wishing me like to one more rich in hope,	C
Featured like him, like him with friends possessed,	D
Desiring this man's art and that man's scope,	C
With what I most enjoy contented least;	D
Yet in these thoughts myself almost despising,	E
Haply I think on thee, and then my state,	F
Like to the lark at break of day arising	E
From sullen earth sings hymns at heaven's gate.	F
For thy sweet love remembered such wealth brings	G
That then I scorn to change my state with kings.	G

As lovers of great music, that amazing art that speaks almost directly to the heart even before it is consciously sensed, we must find its underlying and detailed measurement an act of love. It is precisely the care taken with measuring music that enables different instrumentalists to realize it over and over. And this care is very self-conscious right in the vocabulary used to relate a group of notes: a measure. The calibration of notes as whole, half, quarter, eighth, and continuing factors of fourths makes possible the collaboration of multiple instruments and the glorious richness we call harmonics. The story of the man rushing into a bar across the street from Carnegie Hall brings measurement home. " Fourteen, fifteen—a double Scotch on the rocks please!—eighteen, nineteen, twenty, twenty-one—thanks—twenty-three—what do I owe you?"

"Six fifty. But what's with all the counting?

"Twenty-seven, twenty-eight, twenty-nine—I play tuba in the symphony performing across the street, and I have a 104-beat rest!"

Gulp and out the door.

More flexible than the average concert hall, the theatre is equipped to illustrate richness even with the popular music that so often becomes iconic. In his magnificent first Broadway revival of *South Pacific*, Bartlett Sher virtually staged the moment when the show's overture grows from solo to harmonics. The overture began with the eminently recognizable melody of "Bali Hai" played on a solo wind instrument. Through that moment, the forestage platform extended right to the orchestra pit rail, leaving only a few feet for the conductor to be seen. As soon as the score explodes into the full orchestral harmonics of the piece, that forestage rolled back to reveal the entire orchestra of over thirty members. It was not unusual for the audience to stand for an ovation at this moment, so appealing in its grandeur.

Even a beginning child piano student can suspect that all such theatrics are done with the careful and complete counting dictated by those pesky notes on a five-line staff. That elemental grammar of calculation is gift enough in that it makes music possible in the first place; that it preserves music to be repeated and shared is nothing less than love.

The concert stage celebrates such love in presenting us with the combined musical efforts of quite large orchestral ensembles realizing the very sounds the composers made centuries before. The intensities shared between composer, conductor, instrumentalists, and audience members are all made possible by counted measurement.

But there is another staged celebration of the measured miracle we call music: dance. Music feeds the dance and satisfies that urge everyone feels to up and do something about literally stirring music. The professional dance ensemble, always measuring its leaps, plies, pirouettes, and lifts by counting with the music, doubles for us in "up and doing something" about and with the music.

While the musical theater is often considered *only* a popular art, it has sometimes starkly realized the relationships between performance art categories, all of which are measured. If the reader would suffer the use of yet another classic warhorse from Broadway, the classical Greek understanding of a progress from spoken word to sung word to danced melody could be illustrated. Even Laurie's words leading up to "Out of My Dreams" in *Oklahoma!* are measured so that by the time she sings, the orchestra has played her introduction under the lines and is ready to meet her singing character. It is as if she cannot express everything she is feeling by just speaking. She breaks into song. But one of the most thorny rehearsal problems is precisely when, under her dialog, the orchestra begins to play that intro so that it does truly meet the vocalist when she needs to sing. Even the character may be counting as she speaks her lines.

But it never works. That is to say, the singing of the words expressing her feelings doesn't satisfy her—or us. She needs to do more, and of course, that more is dance. And in *Oklahoma!* what a dance it is. The original choreographer, Agnes de Mille, did not at all feel that ballet was somehow above the musical comedy and plotted a dance sequence in the show that surrealistically tells the story in such a way that even our fears about it are onstage with Laurie's. It is considered one of the bravest and most significant steps in the development of what became the American musical. Like all written music, it can be repeated thanks to the measurement inherent to music. And those same notes, chords, and phrases will cue the dancers realizing Ms. DeMille's concept from eighty years ago.

It is easy to assess the appreciation and rich enjoyment audiences have with formally presented music. There are measurable anticipation and release in the thirteenth through seventeenth measures of Chopin's famous Polonaise in A-flat Major, "The Heroic." And Chopin's instinctive genius sensed what this virtually sensuous experience would be, so he repeats it four measures later in a different key and later an octave higher, and again and again, we hear it echoed because he knows how emotionally provocative it is.

The satisfaction musicians take in performing with their instruments is also very significant. Making music has to be more pleasurable than just listening to it. Coaxing one's instrument into a measured and consonant relationship with other players and instruments must produce the satisfaction guaranteeing the presence of music throughout history. Anyone having had the pleasure of watching and hearing the likes of Lang Lang concertize has few doubts about the artist's love for his instrument and what he can make it do.

The joy of making and hearing music is underlined in the compulsion so many musicians have to come together to make instrumental music for themselves. String ensembles are perhaps the most dramatic cases in point. Even the amateur violinist Einstein, now probably taking harp lessons in the upper reaches, maintained that "Life without playing music is inconceivable for me."

While at Princeton, Einstein and other musicians had an established string ensemble that met regularly, largely for their own pleasure. One of the legendary moments in their history of playing together was when a particular new passage was giving them difficulty and the ensemble stumbled at exactly the same place repeatedly. Exasperated, the leader turned to the great physicist and queried ironically, "Albert! Can't you count?"

9

WORD

IN A LITERATE society, when it comes to taking artifacts for granted, there is perhaps no more overlooked object than the word. Illiterate people overlook words, too, routinely accepting the code hidden in their whistles, groans, hisses, hums, and clicks that one day might get written down. But it is not hard to imagine a double neglect when the sound and its transcription are both overlooked in the haste to communicate. Yes, communication is the paramount goal until the right words cannot be called up. It is then that the hummed scribbles get their due. Partially. There is such an automatic, effortless quality to so much language that the units that make it possible and valuable are nearly invisible. Even the act of writing or keyboarding is so immediate that given words realized in the processes are well-nigh invisible, even though they are being oh-so quietly and quickly sounded—unvoiced, in the brain.

But they are artifacts, both sound and script, even when they are traceable developments in the history of related languages. Poets have long found the music hidden in combinations of the humble syllables, and that poetry has so often found fuller voice with the accompaniment of instrumental music.

Labels and verbal pointing, the beginnings of a child's linguistic ability, words do make contact with outside surroundings. They mean something even if the meaning of meaning in all its arbitrariness is far ahead in the mind's development. With the adult correcting the little recitation, self-imposed quizzes, accompanied by pointing, may include "chair," "light," "baby," and, where there's doubt, perhaps "table?" with the quiz slightly turned on the adult.

No assembly of words about words can be compre hensive without the worldly reflection that is syntax. How the *baby* affects the *chair* and the *table* determine the use of more words: perhaps *climb* and *onto*. And somehow the pointing and labeling give way to a simple monosyllable starting with the teeth and followed by just voiced air: *the*.

To think that this mysterious and wonderful process is repeated in myriad infancies across the globe's collection of over six thousand languages. Then to wonder where the sounds and their connections come from, differentiated and interacted. The most famous solution to the simple matter of translation has to be the Rosetta Stone. Carved in the second century BCE, it was discovered at the end of the eighteenth century CE. When the section written in ancient Greek was seen to refer to the same subject as that written in contemporary Egyptian, the suspicion arose that the same subject was treated in the hieroglyphic section. It was the first breakthrough in a modern understanding of the ancient Egyptian symbols.

The histories of given words are windows into other eras and cultures that have seemed unconnected to the present experience until the logic of the words' formation is realized. The ubiquitous *ma* for *breast, mother*, and the variants like *mammary*, and *amazon*, and the Hindi *pandit*, Sanskrit *pandita*, English *pundit*, might be cases in point.

Yesterday a friend died whom no one would have identified as an artist, least of all an artist with words. Born with a severely cleft palate and inheriting a completely failed surgical attempt to correct the disorder, his life was one of toothless mumbling and sleeping with his tongue hanging out. Until he heard the words of another. And then the mumbling took on an earnestness that could either clear some of the syllables or try to rush over them and blur them even worse.

Because anything like conversation took an immense amount of time and patience, few people ever engaged him. He was left at the edge of all social gatherings, even the most casual. After so many attempts to tell neighbors who he was, he took his place even further from the social edges and was left staring from afar. Alone.

Until someone left their circle and made an effort to talk with him. Words would emerge; syntax not so much. The connectors—forget prepositions and articles—were severely faded. But a verb or noun often provided an emotional base that even called up a more or less proper configuration of the mouth. He slowed way down when he disapproved and could get about four syllables out of ssssshiiiiiiiiiiiiiiiiiitt! To be fair, he could get plenty of time out of an approval with helly-eeeeeeceeessssssssssssss. From there, it was a gradual climb up to recognizing his vocabulary. Probably thirty percent accuracy was tops. The rest was guesswork and emphatic sign language.

Ironically, on the day my friend died, the *Washington Post* ran an article about a tracheotomy patient who had resorted to writing in lieu of trying to speak. Described as delirious, a chief nurse chattered on about how he even wrote nonsense. The patient, concerned about leaving the hospital the next day, wrote out the opening words of the most famous speech in Shakespeare's

Macbeth (5.5.19–20): "Tomorrow…creeps in this petty pace." My friend wouldn't have recognized the quote from Shakespeare, but he would have understood that irony and laughed heartily. Cleft and re-cleft palates are not easy to understand, but ears and minds comprehend perfectly, even the double entendres that make jokes work. This makes the final diagnosis of "severe dementia" extremely hard to accept and too easy a dismissal by professionals without time to hear through the deformity. Just the commonplace ability of getting a joke signals accurate and active mental capacity. So it is that this sad loss of ours yesterday was a joke on us and all our clarity.

Even one hundred years after Shakespeare's life, literacy in England was less than fifty percent. This more than suggests that most of the audiences for the famous plays only heard words. They could not imagine words because they had never seen them, much less memorized them. Emphasis was on *hearing* a play even over *seeing* it. This made for a great mine of verbal comedy based on double meanings. Nonsense and falsehood, commonly referred to as *bs* or BS, was signified by reference to bovine anatomy with "and thereby hangs a tale/tail." (Hear your choice.)

Now, four hundred years after the Bard, literacy finds itself accelerated via electronics to the point of vocabularies of abbreviations much more extensive than the humble BS, BYOB, or MYOB. As it is, LOL, OMG, LMK, and XOXO have sent more than one pre-millennial quizzing on the internet. And "What did we do before the computer and the internet?" has become a rather selfish question given the number of folks who are actually computer illiterate. They indeed make do without the internet and computers day in and day out. To its credit, the current acceleration of literate communications allows ideas to find their form and connections more rapidly and plentifully than before. The difference in time between a thought's formation and a written word's has been blessedly lessened. "No sooner thought than written" is almost a possibility.

Besides acceleration, computer filing and recall possibilities have made possible a mammoth editing phenomenon, allowing for great quantities of information to be available to eyes and fingertips in seconds. The Apple "library reference desk" known as Siri makes such information, instantly gleaned from seemingly infinite resources, seem a little more human.

And the humanity that is language, humans speaking to one another or writing to one another, must never be at risk. The adage "Oh, she's not speaking to me!" speaks volumes in that very *not speaking*. Such proclamations testify that our speech is our key to association with one another. Informal chat, in particular, can unlock our too often uptight personalities and render friendship and even new insights possible. "Shootin' the breeze" and its variants, regardless of how they're interpreted, label informal conversations that often solve problems, ease awkwardness, and enlighten the mysterious.

One of the most accessible displays of the intimate connection between language and the humanity of accepted values is in the words of Shakespeare's most intelligent coward, Falstaff. Left alone on the battlefield in *Henry IV, Part One*, 129 ff, the old knight confronts his own honor. He has a commission he knows, and that is to be ready to die for his king. No one hearing Falstaff's almost clever rationalization of *honor, word, air* believes he believes himself. But even in such comedy, there is a jarring image of the intimacy of word and self as character. Honoring one's word is a cooler rendition of such intimacy, but again the proximity of person and spoken image is highlighted.

In the struggle to express intangibles, such as a virtue, the randomness of language emerges. Who says those two sounds really reflect what is meant by *honor*? Etymology be damned. The sound and the virtue got together somewhere at some time. Why? And how brave was the apostle John, that young guy who apparently took a long time growing up and thinking before he okayed a beloved hymn for the preface to his gospel. "In the beginning was the word" (1:1).

So, Sir John Falstaff, William "Shakes" Shakespeare, and John "Beloved" Zebedee walk into a baptistry. As the other two are immediately taken with the décor, Sir John whines.

Sir John: Shakes, I thought you were taking us to a bar!

Shakes: I said, "a baptistry," Sir John. Didn't I say that, Beloved?

Beloved: You did, Shakes. But in fairness, there is now a tavern in Southwark called "The Baptistry."

Sir John: Yeah, but important things happen in bars and taverns. I remember in Eastcheap once—

Shakes: Careful, Sir John. You're implying im portant things don't happen in baptistries.

Beloved: But Shakes, in fairness, important things happen in taverns. That's how Sir John met Mistress Quickly.

Shakes and Sir John: *(In unison)* How do you know that?

Beloved: I read a lot, you know.

Sir John: *(To Shakes)* Just how much does he know?

Beloved: So, why did you bring us to a baptistry?

Shakes: *(Indicating the carved legend around font)* I wanted us to see this.

Sir John: *(Reading)* "In the beginning was the word..." Hmmmm. *(As if saying it for the first time)* What is that word?

Shakes: *(To Beloved, somewhat triumphantly)* You wrote that!

Beloved: No, I didn't. *(Pointing at Sir John)* But you said that!

Shakes: C'mon. Everyone knows those words, and here are the numbers locating it: John one, one.

Sir John: *(Now in his own world)* What is a number?

Beloved: It's *Henry IV, Part One*, five, one, one hundred and thirty-four.

Sir John: Now, that's a number!

Beloved: Actually, I didn't write that hymn opening my gospel. By that time, we all knew certain poems and songs by heart. All I did was say it was a good idea to open with.

Shakes and Sir John: *(Together)* Well, what's it mean?

Beloved: You know, Sir John. Air.

Sir John: *(Recalling his line)* Oh, right! Genius!

Shakes: So, in the beginning was air?

Sir John: *(Still lost in his self-review)* Just genius!

Beloved: Don't forget, air can be shaped, Shakes, and words shape ideas, and ideas reflect spirits. God is a whirlwind of complexity. That main office is a busy place. But simply put, this word is Jesus. And everything God made, he made in the name of Jesus. So, before there was creation, in the beginning, there was just the word that will become Jesus.

Sir John: That's it! That's it! I told you about taverns. At the Mermaid the other night, Sir Toby Belch explained all of that: it's all one. It's all one! Genius. Genius! God and creation are all one in Jesus. Oh, Sir Toby.

Shakes: I'm embarrassed.

Beloved: No need. We're all right. We just have to live a good-enough life to understand the words. *(Looking at Falstaff)* And I think we do.

Of course, actors playing their roles know that they can spin circles with words, and in the centers of those circles, they can teach us. But what of us who are not teaching or acting? How do we use our words?

In a very real sense, words help us keep the place in our thinking. Most certainly, we can imagine and wonder and think without words, but they make it much easier for us to direct the traffic of all those images and connections. Even if we're not aware of them, we are constantly talking to ourselves in words we can just about see so that when it's necessary to write them or articulate them in speech, they are right at hand. Imagined words strengthen and clarify one another and facilitate speech.

That wonderful query between close friends, "What are you thinking?" bespeaks trust and belief in the respondent's ability to formulate his thinking: trust in a certainty they have a mutual right to know each other's thoughts and belief because past answers to the question have been articulate. The question might be rephrased: "I can't read your mind; what are you thinking?" suggesting that the friendship is one that presumes such openness.

Happily there are occasions when thousands of mute spectators can read a lone performer's mind. The late clown, Lou Jacobs, used to silently engage hordes of quiet children sitting in Madison Square garden with his "rabbit hunting" routine. The kids put the scenario together instantly. The clown was carrying a gun and a "rabbit" (actually his fox terrier wearing rabbit ears) was following him. When he stopped in the center of the ring and mimed intense looking—hunting?—for rabbits, the kids obliged by screaming as one, "Behind you!" even growing impatient enough to repeat their shout. But then, when Lou, following orders, turned and spotted the "rabbit" he knelt on one knee and took dead aim. My how the children's mood changed with a very sad and universal cry from all over the arena, "Noooooooooooooo!" Drama at its finest and leanest, all the way to the end when the little dog faked being dead, escaped the gunny sack he was put in and followed the master clown out of the performance area.

So, words can be used for more than the illustration of thoughts or hazy matters of faith; they are also instruments of love. Like the works of art they so often are, they can be preserved for later readers. One of the most celebrated acts of literary love involves an early seventeenth-century triangle: John Heminges, Henry Condell, and William Shakespeare. Heminges and Condell had been very active members of the King's Men, Shakespeare's acting company, and after his death in 1616, they realized that the treasured playscripts that had passed through their hands so usefully should be collected and preserved. By 1623, their efforts emerged as *The First Folio* of *Mr. William Shakespeares Comedies, Histories, and Tragedies.* Half of the works had not seen print before.

It is obviously an act of love that brought about the immense collection in the first place; it is often overlooked that making the treasured works available to unknown millions in unimagined centuries was itself a magnificent act of love for the rest of us. And that we can laugh at poor old Falstaff, thrill and weep with Juliet, rage at Iago, judge Richard III, or lament the wasted brilliance of Hamlet is all because of words. And such words. One hesitates to juxtapose the present words with even the names of Shakespeare's characters, so elegant are the settings that gave us those personages. All words.

Sadly, words can work opposite effects to the clarity and honesty they enjoy as bridges of love. Truth is only about half of the payload any composition may be expected to carry. Maybe few of us can handle all the truth all the time. Two days ago, the president of the United States severed connections with several polling firms because they weren't reporting what he wanted to hear. Not unexpectedly, it was during this official's term that the notion of "fake news" became popular. The truth is, words can lie. So, if a reporter can save his job by delivering wrong words, the temptation is there. What an insult. The undercurrent conversation in such false contexts begins, "You can't handle what is happening, so I won't let my words reflect it." And so words, those intimate and trusted markers of our thoughts and feelings, are allowed to betray themselves in scenarios for which they have a completely alternative script almost at tongue.

Less offensive might be the misuse of words in such a way that they promise more than the speaker can really deliver or even live up to. Blowhards have often been characterized as comic figures, but there are probably few putdowns of fakery that outperform the following: "In promulgating your esoteric conjugations or articulating your superficial sentimentalities, please beware of supercilious ostentations of erudite vacuity.

Without being too introversive, any writer has to be thankful that the last paragraph could be written at all and with so little attention given the words themselves. There is an almost immediate translation continuously enacted in the brain of symbol to reality or remembered image. Language about experienced reality can only happen with an abundance of time and freedom from a detailed schedule—like during recess time, when the wonders of memory and imagination can emerge and reconnect in new memories and new images.

10

ART

FOR SO MUCH of the public, art gets a tough rep. It seems too special, apart, and aloof. But that's probably only because most folks aren't artists or don't think they're artistic. However, everyone makes even joyful use of the artistic output around us: architecture, photography, background music, and clothing design, to name only a few areas that affect us regularly.

Notice that everyday artistic encounters might not even involve sculpture, painting, or museums. That is not to say the influences we do enjoy—commercial applications in advertising, for instance, are not inspired by such classic instances of art.

To be an artist, whether commercial or classical, is an amazing privilege: rendering the gift of being to something that hasn't existed. Such genius borders on magic and evidences humanity's considerable power. Through the attraction of outright beauty, or the clarity of an insight, art sets out to make truth irresistible. And we find ourselves arguing with the Greeks and Pontius Pilate over "What is truth?"

That question is not only provocative; it is brave, hearty, and artistic itself. The truth is that truth is nearly impossible to define. Usually, we wind up (for a time) accepting a quasi-sociological definition of how widespread an experience or opinion might be. Next to "What is being?" it may be the most philosophical probe in human thought.

Artists don't set out to make the truth. They just want to make something new by combining elements they know in a different way. Beauty and relationship is their guide; truth is a later, perhaps accidental, discovery. Thus, a coarse piece of cloth becomes a dreamy afternoon sojourn in a park, a block of solid marble yields sinewy flesh, and a catchy children's nursery tune is rendered the spine of a classic orchestration. Self-consciousness during these processes takes a very back seat in the forward thrust of production. Most often, a detailed and complete rendering of what is happening is nowhere in the artist's imagination. Deliberately she leaves herself open to discovering relationships in the medium she has chosen.

"What gave you the idea for that?" is usually an

answerable question. "What inspired you to develop that detail?" not so much. We only act on inspiration; seldom do we examine it. That might even seem presumptuous or unworthy. Enough to act on it, seize it, and run. Given the advances of neuronic study, the subject itself seems literally fraught with electricity. More connections are being made than consciousness can grasp. And so the artist paints, carves, or writes notes on a staff, echoing what he imagines. We have art, and that is good, and that seems enough.

Until we disagree. How can such an ugly expression as "Hell is other people" be art? You can't be serious about *The Scream*. Sartre and Munch are both masters at arresting our attention. In these instances, the line from *No Exit* and the painting of a distressed human with a rebellious (screaming?) nature behind him, we really do sit up and pay attention. Parts of our everyday misery and angst are rendered in a form that is not only shocking but resolving. One dimension of our everyday tensions over social misfires and human panic is that we ignore them. They do not get addressed outrightly. The repressed impulses behind "I so want to tell him to go to hell" or "I'm so upset I could scream" stay repressed. And then an artist comes along and with a strikingly—yes, beautiful—form, lets us release the pressure.

That second syllable of *inspiration* too handily

invokes a near-religious undercurrent for such discussions until we remember that its root meaning is really *breath*. Maybe "What inspired you" just means "What were you breathing?" but that translation gets (ahem!) troublesome, too. "What gave you the *idea* for such a form?" might have to suffice. In any case, such questions recognize that the artist has come up with something new, surprising, and beautiful in such a way as to arrest one's attention. Instances of such power command our time. A friend visiting Paris for the first time told his guide that what he really wanted to see were the French impressionists. Of course, she took him to the Centre Pompidou, and there among all the celebrated floating canvas images, he surprised himself by singling out a nearly mathematical crisp cubist piece by Picasso. Needless to say, his attention had been arrested by such obviously calculated form. It was definitely a spiritual experience, and well, it took his breath away. He forgot the formal impressionism.

Perhaps some of the truly great instances of art through history have come in combined forms, such as those in architecture. With constructive shaping, even carpenters hammer out sculptures, stonemasons are obviously closer to actually carving, and the décor lavished on such structures may involve both sculpture and painting. Often these hybrid works of art are commissioned for public places of very lively governmental traffic, the exhibition of art itself, familial display of wealth, or in commemoration of important events.

One of the world's most celebrated structures, and justifiably a wonder of the modern world, is the Taj Mahal of Agra, in Uttar Pradesh, India. Commissioned by a Mughal, Shah Jahan, in 1631, it is both a love story and a celebration of life in death. Accordingly, the Taj Mahal is a white marble jewel box of a mausoleum, and Mumatz Mahal's tomb is in its very center. She was Jahan's favorite wife, a Persian princess who died giving birth to their fourteenth son. The raw statistics underlying the actual construction—twenty-two thousand laborers working twelve years and a thousand elephants hauling materials deliberately collected from all over Asia to a forty-two-acre complex—are overwhelming but fall to the realm of oblivion at one's first visit to the site. Even the approach to the actual mausoleum is designed for a gradual involvement of the visitor's senses and emotions. Nothing was to interfere with the vista of the piece itself. To this end, the property on the north side of the Yamuna River is controlled so that no architectural structure can compromise this vista. Of course, the visual poetry of the domes themselves is overwhelming enough. The symmetry of all structures in view is anything but boring because, even at a distance, the extravagant decorative detail is discernible. If anything, it is a very busy and holy symmetry thanks to that detail.

And that detail is what pulls the visitor's eyes, heart, and spirit forward. Those so impressive statistics flash by, but only momentarily as the sacred quality and content of the calligraphy (that just has to be from the Qur'an) on the expansive white marble corrects your focus. Perhaps a guide will assure you that indeed some of the calligraphy is from the Qur'an and some from Persian poetry. But within reach of fingertips, the calligraphy stuns with its own magic: it is inlaid with semi-precious and precious stone. You're seeing malachite from Russia, jade from China, turquoise from Tibet, lapis-lazuli from Afghanistan, rubies from Sri Lanka, yellow amber from Burma, and cat's eyes from Egypt.

The inlaying process is itself a feat of intricate sculpture, the exact cut into the marble for the colored stone's secure placement. In the instances at eye level where the stones have fallen out, one can see the recesses and the carver's tool marks. Millions of stones? Millions of carved recesses—everything is dominated, of course, by the sensual curvature of the so-called onion dome, a Persian-influenced motif of so many Muslim mosques.

One takes for granted the four minarets towering around the main structure. Then a chance angle of sight or a purposeful photograph reveals the slight angle at which each minaret is tilted away from the main mausoleum. Thus, a collapse would have a given tower falling outward from the main dome rather than onto it. Even in the engineering of this marvel, life in death, order in destruction, seem present.

The largest church building in the world is St. Peter's Basilica in Rome. Its chief architectural component is, again, a vaulted dome, but in adjacent structures such as the Sistine Chapel, much of the upper architecture in and around the ceiling is a feat of tromp l'oeil painting by Michelangelo, himself primarily a sculptor. In the nearby titular church of the Society of Jesus, the major interior effect of a vaulted dome is another trick: the entire inside of the "dome" is an illusion painted on a flat ceiling.

If visual art communicates so vividly with us, the imagined phrases of a musical composition stagger us as we try to comprehend the imaginations that "hear" what does not yet exist. Of course, one can ask where the idea for any art comes from, but "hearing" with the imagination seems near ghostly. Recording such imaginations and reproducing them with instruments designed for the purpose seem logical follow-ups to the "from nowhere" instances of invention.

A singing friend of mine knows nothing about the scales, the keyboard, or writing music, yet he invents melodies as readily as he creates the words they celebrate. More than that, he performs this music in public with the help of instrumentalist friends. His may be an imagination worth noting for the source of those phrased and varied sounds we call music. A rich sampling of his creative ability is to be found in the lyrics of his "My Winter Symphony." He has made a prayer out of his unhappiness with Midwestern weather.

> Down inside
> Our lady Winters throat,
> The summer scrounges
> For his winter coat.
> Abandoned mind he
> Silly slipped away,
> Suffering from all
> The pain he gained.
>
> Lord, play my winter symphony.
> Lord, play my winter symphony.
> I feel the earth going down,
> But I'll just blow her a kiss.
> Lord, play my winter symphony.
> Lord, play my winter symphony.
>
> I'm a rusty needle in my
> Father's vein.
> I'm a salty tear that puts my
> Mother to shame.

Dear lord, reserve me
A spot up above.
Please let the pain be,
Let it all be done.

Lord, play my winter symphony.
Lord, play my winter symphony.
I feel the earth going down,
But I'll just blow her a kiss.
Lord, play my winter symphony.
Lord, play my winter symphony.

I fancy a boy, but he don't quite fancy me.
I'll still rule the world,
Whoever and me.
I fancy a girl, but she don't quite fancy me.
I'll still rule the world,
Whoever and me.

Whoever and me,
Winter symphony.

                              Kylle St. Trail

Sung in his delicate falsetto, the prayer is both
humble and demanding: humble in that he doesn't
yet rule the world, demanding in that he really wants
his symphony played. Until the words are sung, or

imagined as sung, they are poetry. The musical relationship between syllables and sung notes is just about a zero-to-one breakthrough. The memory of musical phrases, like the memory of verbal phrases, may be the secret along with the developed courage to actually try out any number of musical phrases in the ear of the imagination.

Of course, the ability to imagine notes on staves and written music helps the creation of music immensely. Even so, as with all great art, the finished musical product is much more than remembered moments, parts, or passages. A lifetime of training an artist's neuronic trajectories, that is, a lifetime of following one's preferences and reinforcing what one typically resonates with in the preferences of models and teachers, must be the answer. Like so much else in human endeavor, we won't be absolutely sure where art originates until science—in its own artistic ways—reveals more about the workings of the brain. And no matter how precisely satisfied a composer is with his work, once it is released or published, he has no control over what it will spark in another listener. Regardless of what Chopin was imagining as he wrote that famous Polonaise in A-Flat Major, "The Heroic," measures twelve through seventeen or the later nineteen measures of descending, left-handed octaves reminded Liszt and a student of an equine stampede!

It hardly lessens the quality or intensity of dance to recognize its source in music. It is precisely a relief of that pressure we feel to "up and do something" about the music. In the studio, a teacher or choreographer will have already realized the form she thinks the music calls for. If she has not realized original moves, she will have memorized those of a previous performance. Dance has a language and shorthand of its own, and what seems to the layman a whirlwind of images can be recorded in a specialized stenography.

Yes, there can be dance without music, and that type of event always spurs two questions. Is there anything like music going through the dancer's imagination as she executes the steps? Is not such dancing tantamount to mime? As it happens, there is a considerable amount of mimed storytelling in classical dance. That's how we find out Siegfried's mother wants him married in Swan Lake. And poor old Drosselmeyer has to grow tired in his *Nutcracker* role, which combines the magic of Santa Claus and the effort of a stage manager all communicated through mime.

Given the importance of the artistic word, its realization in music, and its influence on bodily expression in dance, are there instances beyond musical comedy where all of these expressions happen at the same time? Happily, yes. The famed dance sequences of opera soar with the combined powers of their charged musical and dramatic sources. The "Toreador Song" from *Carmen,* the Act 2 entr'acte and chorus from *Eugene Onegin,* and "Zitti, zitti, moviamo a vendetta" from *Rigoletto* are a few examples.

So much happens because of the spoken word. The theater—whether a basement space or grand opera house—seems a space developed to protect and celebrate everything the word can inspire. And before there were theaters after Europe's so-called Dark and Middle Ages, there were "occasions" of theater: gatherings in inn yards, for instance, and public spaces accommodating a platform and an audience. It is as if our genes demand such recitations about who we are and where we came from. Of course, the most cherished of developments from the Early Modern English era was the talent of William Shakespeare. He was ten or eleven years old when the first permanent theater was built in the Shoreditch area of London. Ten years later, he vanishes from all records of his whereabouts, only to turn up in the now popular and expanded crowd of London's actors, playwrights, and theater managers.

There is such an abundance of evidence that the man who became Shakespeare the playwright began as an actor; the one-time penchant for attributing his works to others has evanesced in deference to scholarship. And by the time there are records of his presence in London, he is co-writing *Henry VI, Part Two,* probably with another playwright, Kit Marlowe. By this time, he is an acknowledged actor, having performed in another contemporary poet's plays. We know he was in Ben Jonson's *Sejanus His Fall* and later in *Everyman in His Humor* Every element of theatrical possibility became part of his artistic arsenal so that by the time he was writing a virtual masque for *A Midsummer Night's Dream* he just might have been forecasting what we will come to know as grand opera.

Whatever the nature of God, the overall power of art's creativity in whatever Art is might easily make for a component of the godly. There is an admitted force that effects change throughout existence. In her achievement of a new form, is not the artist participating in the life and work of a force we can call God?

To execute progression from the sublime to the ridiculously sublime, any discussion of the performing arts must include a form that existed throughout the twentieth century. This artistic realization brought its gallery, studios, musicians, and grand theater to any empty field or unused lot near or in any town that wanted it. Commercial to the extreme, it caught its patrons off guard, but only where they were. Dress, downtown traffic, expensive tickets, and the foreknowledge that costly education provided were irrelevant. This art met us where we were and stretched our imaginations about what we might want to be or do. And the next morning, artists, galleries, and theater were gone. The field was empty. The circus had come to our town.

For most of a century and a half, the tented circus was an institution throughout the United States. By 1950, having continuously expanded and improved on its European forbears, it was huge, with a big top seating twelve thousand spectators, a menagerie more complete than some metropolitan zoos, a sideshow with near-outrageous wonders of anatomy in celebrated display, and the main event of music, acrobats, parades, comics, trained animals, and, early on, even staged scenes of operatic scale titled "Cleopatra" and "Aida." But twenty years into the twenty-first century, more and more fields and lots are empty all the time, and all but the physical and comic artistry has vanished. (Thankfully, very skilled acrobats and other former circus performers now teach their gifts to young people all over the world.) In general, art used primarily for entertainment must face the cruel reality of entertainment competition. The marriage of technology and popular amusement has provided twenty-four-seven distraction right in the palms of our hands. Who needs to go to a field?

As we struggle with traffic, limited crowds, and high ticket prices to partake in the myriad of art we have at galleries, concert halls, and theaters, there is a mammoth gift we somehow miss. It is completely tangible and human: artists, their talents, and their willingness to work at sharing those gifts. And the gift of artistic sensibility is part of all complete humanity. Creativity is a dynamic participation in being itself.

(Now, how did we get back to the sublime?)

11

FOOD

OF THE FUNDAMENTALS of living, there can be none more necessary than eating. In earlier stages of civilization, when we were regular parts of other animals' food chains, it might have been more obvious to humans. Organisms simple and complex must be fed. And what a complex of interdependency that sets up, especially with the advent of business and the profit motive. Good and bad nutrition hang out in advertising firms, which respond to the stock market. And ready availability replaces the centuries-old reflex of "stocking up." Sadly, a culture's wealth too often varies inversely with its nutritional health.

Science, such as organic chemistry and nutritional biology, seems ready to come to the rescue as long as it can protect itself—and us—from the gluttony of the marketplace. Fortunately, there are enough sound answers to the question "What is good for my diet?" that any reasonably educated and informed person can remain healthy. But what about the uneducated and uninformed when they come up against hunger's calls and the readiness of fast food and slick shelving? What about the immense contingent of the populace, especially single men, who know nothing about cooking? In certain colonies of low-income housing, one expects social services to post recipes for boiling water. "I don't cook!" can be an anthem for a tired housewife or as over-the-top male braggadocio, which sees food preparation as feminine or gay.

The memory of Mom's cookin' comes to the rescue so often—"Oh, man, we loved it when she made that"—and recalled glimpses of kitchen procedures can lead or drive one to a pot or two, some fresh vegetables, and the stove. Trial and error add the seasoning, and taste passes judgment. Cynicism aside, there is enough agreement on the right stores and aisles to shop in that a minimum of goodwill and hunger will support nutritional health.

Consistency and scheduling seem as important to health as dietary choices. One can amass the most medically approved stockpile of fresh foods and totally derail its benefits by succumbing to "I just don't feel hungry" or "Man, am I famished!" syndromes too, uh, regularly. That is not to say that the complex organisms of the body shouldn't be listened to. Perhaps the "too much" or "not enough" signals are being tripped. But instant remedial attention may not be called for as much as a modification at the next meal. Habit, good or less good, is always at the ready with human behavior. An extra snack today and tomorrow can soon lead to a caloric overload, with minimum awareness.

In general, habits should be a fairly regular concern in human behavior. In fact, habitual review of one's habits seems a requisite for good physical health.

Of course, protein is a major concern in any diet. Somehow, Americans have learned this too well. On average, they consume twice as much protein as they require. How one gets the required amount of protein is another story. Americans haven't learned terribly much about the panoply of protein sources there are besides red meat. Many don't even know what a legume is, let alone how good it might be for them. The difference between nuts, seeds, and grains can often seem tantamount to graduate work.

Avoiding unwanted and unnecessary carbohydrates can be as difficult as knowing what and where they are. Often the primary textbook is right in our hands, but we don't take advantage of it. Pulling a jar of peanut butter off the shelf because "Hey, peanuts are good protein for you!" and a particular brand because "Hey, it's a lot cheaper than Skippy's!" misses the first lesson in nutrient research. Finding the back of the label and identifying the dense paragraph of ingredients as well as the comparative list of *DVs* (i.e., *Daily Values*) is very important. Knowing that the ingredients are listed in descending order of amount included in the product is even more important. Sure enough, peanuts are listed first, so the chief ingredient in the jar is peanuts. How about the second ingredient? Sugar. Not good. Carbs. Calories. Addictive (makes you want to eat the whole jar). Or is sugar wearing one of its more scientific disguises? Dextrose? High-fructose corn syrup? Fun, eh? So, we look for one ingredient: peanuts. It's there, and it's pricier.

Familiarity with how food is prepared can be valuable even if one chooses to remain a consumer instead of a preparer. Hummus, that tasty, adaptable, handy little spread that shows up so often as an elegant dip among the hors d'oeuvres has a very humble beginning: garbanzo beans. Make it yourself with your blender and some spicy accents. Terrific. Cheap. A legume, and that means protein. Be sure you know that garbanzos have another name: chickpeas. Ground up dry, they make a healthy flour and then all kinds of pasta, pancakes, and waffles.

Peru, that magic Andean adventure with Machu Picchu and coca leaves, taught the world so successfully about one of its seeds that for a while, no one in that nation could afford quinoa (KEEN-wa). It is a complete protein and an inexpensive, easy-to-prepare substitute for rice and pasta.

Education about food and food preparation comes to so many haphazardly: a chance conversation with a friend, overheard chatter on a television cooking show, or downright study if there's a free minute when a nutrition magazine shows up. Formal physical education curricula might include what the body needs to train well. Any sign of commercial sponsorship or product-pushing should be a flag as possibly biased and not entirely objective. An example of such pushing is the very frequent online promise of a perfect body given the exclusion of, say, "These three vegetables" but the inclusion of "My original invention after years of research: Supplement X."

Basically, the rule might be to eat what one needs and avoid what one really doesn't need. After the basics, labeled ingredients become required reading for everyone. Yes, I need seasoning; no, I don't need sugar or most of the array of ingredients ending in -*ose*. Fresh fruits and their fruct*ose* are an exception here. I must become ancient Greek and be convinced that whatever my diet, "moderation is best."

Whatever a diet consists of, it costs; it has a price. Personal budgeting obviously reflects current monetary

and commercial worth. But there can be more important prices hidden to ordinary consumers. How much
is known about sources for products eaten? The incon-
venience of an empty shelf row in a supermarket is very
minor. What about truckload deliveries that no longer
have a given product? Or entire sections of warehouse
floors lacking it? Or harvesters unable to find it because
its ingredients no longer make enough profit? Why has
profit fallen? Is it because the earth finds it more and
more difficult to produce the ingredient? Is that what
the grocery clerk meant when asked why her store no
longer carried a certain brand of health supplement
based on kelp? "We could no longer guarantee that the
harvesting methods were sustainable." Was she reporting that corporate was a bit Greek? Might *moderation*
include *sustainability*?

Basically, the earth runs out of stuff, space, and citizens. The famous saying found in the book of Hebrews,
"We have not here a lasting city," must be understood
globally. We have not here a lasting planet with unlim-
ited resources.

No matter how much health a given species of food
can promise, given items right off the produce display
can kill; think apples, kale, celery, or blueberries. The
conventional growing method practiced widely in
cultivating such items (and many others on the so-
called "dirty dozen" list—cf. Environmental Working

Group's *Consumer Guides*) involves "protecting them" from pests with the aid of toxic chemicals. The effects of such "care" cannot be simply washed off. What to do? Enter the organically grown produce. The price differential is minimal, but there is definitely an increase for the organic items.

Perhaps better known is the sad story of crowded feeder lots and meats harvested with serious overloads of antibiotics to protect livestock from dangerous fecal infections. Passed on to us, such antibiotics can immunize us from the desired effects of antibiotics in the first place. Repulsive as such medical conditions may seem, concern should not be lost for the amount of fat artificially produced by feeder lots. "Pasture-raised" has now become a recognized preferred category in market meat departments. The same type of distinction has been developed to describe eggs and poultry that have been cultivated under healthier conditions. Even such preferences as "wild-caught," describing a source for some varieties of fish, have become significant in supermarkets. Cultivated, "fish farm" products are not as appreciated.

There is another concern affecting diet that bears only indirectly on the health of the consumer, and that is the life of animals. The popular emergence of *veg-etarianism* and *veganism* reflects a broadening concern for the welfare of animals on the planet and a questioning of how necessary such protein is for human health. And aside from that comparative protein quest, a vegetarian or vegan individual has set out from a basic philosophical question: is it kind (humane, moral) to deliberately cultivate and harvest meat and/or animal products if and when, in a culture like ours, such cultivation is totally unnecessary? Broadening awareness of modern livestock industry conditions at the same time as a growing appreciation for animal perception only prompts such considerations. Whatever the outcome of these social concerns, their required abstention from meat and animal produce has to be more grounded and meaningful than various religious abstentions.

Besides the nutritional and biological concern driving our pursuit of diet, there is a psychological dimension to eating that can affect overall well-being, digestion, and physical health. That dimension might suitably be called the dining dimension. With the individualization of our society, insular attachment through cell phones, and the lack of interaction with those immediately around us, the ritual of meals is very often neglected. Eating is done on the run via fast food, almost snuck lunch breaks in the solitude of one's workspace, and often omitted altogether. In this last sense, fast-food culture has virtually outrun us. Even social gatherings find themselves "ordering out" with the excuse that there just isn't time to prepare food. Absent in such situations is the comfort and relaxation of actually using the home kitchen, knowing the ingredients of a meal firsthand, anticipating the smells and flavors, and actually serving the various dishes and drinks. All of this is far more than the customary rituals now facing difficulty in remaining part of our culture. It is obviously far from being necessary since there are the less personal avenues. Running behind the entire process is the remembered energy and warmth of an intense act of love: feeding one's friends.

The humanity of a *conversation*, literally the *turning* of a subject *with* someone else, when it is the setting and ambiance of a meal, subtly reminds us that we are always in need of more than organic nutrition. We also live on thoughts, acceptance, and insight, those intangible movements of the brain that we attribute to mysteries of the "heart" and "soul." Truth be told, such intangibles in the atmosphere of a meal ensure more effective digestion and absorption of the physical substances we ingest.

Relaxing with a drink and hors d'oeuvres before the main meal is served is tantamount to ensuring an ambiance of friendship, a free exchange of ideas, and the warmth of love. Even the expected coolness and distance of a businessmen's dinner meeting are under-taken with the hope that the positive, human strength in outreach can result in new ideas for advanced developments.

"Hey, Charlie. Let's get together for a drink Friday night. Whaddaya say?" No matter where the club or bar is or how good the stock, the operative idea/word in such an unceremonious, non-academic statement is *together.* And while Charlie may understand—even hope!—that the occasion will involve more than one drink, it is not the beverage that keys the meet-up. Charlie is valuable and can sense that he is precisely because he has been addressed this way. Such a shared drink is shared humanity. While the chemical effects of alcohol may reduce inhibition (*in vino veritas*), that is not the primary goal of the invitation. Another class of question introduces such a meeting: "Hey, Mortimer! Let's get drunk tonight!" Notice that there isn't much time for anticipation and that the stated goal of intoxi-cation is upfront. This is not a quest for more life, love or not. It's a ritualistic shutting down.

How completely human is the warm and gener-ous "I was wondering if you'd like to come over to the house for dinner sometime next week." What needs are promised nourishment here? Often one can sense in her eagerness for such an occasion just how "starved" she may be, and she hasn't missed a meal all week. But she hasn't been feeding all of herself.

Whether or not eating involves the so-human enrichment of "going to dinner" or the less social private meal, any eater automatically becomes a member of a group he never sees: a group that keeps him alive. Cultivating and harvesting the stocks of food it takes to fill grocery shelves and household pantries and tables employs a vast and varied army of laborers. While some of these forces may be skilled middle-class citizens protected in their positions by the equivalent of labor unions and their own scarcity, so many others, fifty to seventy percent of farm laborers, find themselves in slave conditions. Because such labor is severe with hardships, it is cheap; because it is cheap, no one wants it; because no one wants it, it is always available, and on the circle goes, trampling the health and well-being of so many. Some cheap laborers, if not a majority, cannot represent their conditions and would-be rights publicly because they are not legal citizens of the nation they feed. It is as if they live under the ground they nurture. Regardless of the political climate hovering over their migratory status, they are, in fact, slaves, and often don't even know it. Thankfully, there are exceptions. I have a friend who operates a farm in Half Moon Bay, California, with the help of the eager labor of homeless and/or jobless people. The produce they harvest on Abundant Grace is for the homeless and hungry.

Sikh temple feeding thousands a day for free, Delhi, India

And we sit down to dinner with our friends. Under our carefully arranged flatware may be fine linen or an elegant placemat on a highly polished wood surface. Candles may reflect themselves in polished glassware. The very fresh and colorful salad has already been served and virtually sings its health and happiness. The casual conversational hum continues through seating that enjoys the grace of manners and even etiquette casually enacted. There is a moment of welcome from the host and then, so often, a formal or not-so-formal call to some kind of prayerful thanksgiving for the food "we are about to receive."

And so *they* sit down to dinner. It is dusk, and

there is only one lightbulb. Heated canned soup is on the menu, but it has been fortified and increased with some fresh beets from the outside fields and several potatoes in accord with treasured habitual recipes from the homeland. Faheem is crying loudly because he is hungry, and Maryam is whining because Damyan is teasing her. There is scolding and then an enforced gathering at the image of the Madonna to light her candles. There is a rush to the rough board table and overturned crate benches. Mother knows how to cook from almost nothing. She is an artist but sits aside from the meal to nurse Faheem. Adult conversation centers around the very audible weather outside and the possibility of no work tomorrow. That would mean no money. More whining because Maryam and Damyan have to wait longer for some shoes. (The pesticide used on the strawberries outside has begun to burn their feet.) A moment to thank Mother and Our Father in Heaven. Mother knows how to cook from almost nothing, but Manolada in West Peloponnese is no Juba, South Sudan, for her.

And so *the world* sits down to dinner, all seven and a half billion of us, more or less every day. And so the earth feeds us, more or less every day. Until it's less? Everywhere? Perhaps for too long, the consumers knew nothing of conservation. And even cultivated conversation centered only on consumption, not the blessed cycle of giving back—even to Mother Earth, who, of course, knows how to cook from almost nothing.

Until she can't.

12

ANIMALS

AMONG THOSE WHO gather daily for the cosmic cuisine are our ancestors and cousins, the animals. Dietary customs and relative etiquette notwithstanding, as long as carnivorous predators are identified and under control, we are a family. It's easy to tell: world consciousness never conceives of planetary animal life without taking all of us into consideration. Legislative oversight now includes all of us, from the tenured professor of literature to the mountain lion lost in a Milwaukee neighborhood. Blood pressures rise worldwide when some rich hobbyist can't rest until she fells a giraffe on a paid hunting expedition. News that Botswana has legalized the culling of their elephant population with a proposed sale of meat for pet food has broken more than elephant hearts/brains. While we may be wrestling with the details of what *closeness* means, it could be that the animal kingdom, including the human species, is now closer than ever before.

The not-always-scientific concept of species is a major stumbling block in appreciating just how inclusive the animal kingdom is. Accepting the higher apes as ancestors of man (with measured indignation to be sure) seems to be easier than sending holiday good wishes to turkey cousins. Yet might there be more than a chuckling sensitivity over the comic greeting card with a healthy turkey carrying a picket sign that reads "Eat Beef"?

As with everything that suggests measurability, sheer numbers do complicate our daily meals. Why are there so many cows and turkeys (and pigs, chickens, and sheep) taking up room at the table? Nothing in nature compares with the reproductive plethora of so-called domestic animals. (Are mice domestic?) We could be at a moment in our history when we blush just a bit when we admit, while passing the salad to a handsome steer, that we have to have something *on* the table if we're going to have this many *at* the table. And as long as the human menu includes animal flesh, the breeder lots and poultry cages will perdure.

Human dietary consciousness has, fortunately, risen to merit scientific studies of just where protein can come from and how much is needed. There is now less acceptance of the opinion that bovines alone can convert vegetable life into protein. Significant percentages of curious and informed shoppers have expressed interest in so-called vegetarian and vegan support from their merchandisers. And even within those ranks, there are refined concerns over processed food as distinct from the freshly combined ingredients of expanded home cooking.

Aside from questions about the dietary use of other animals, social sensitivity has arisen noticeably about the mere use of animals.

[*Disclaimer: This writer is fully aware that writing on such a subject as an eighty-year-old lifetime circus fan and former circus director incurs a risk of seriously limited data and potential bias toward the subject. But oh, the memories and imaginings. Bring on recess!*]

Anyone who has ever worked closely with an animal, whether training a housepet, saddling a horse, or feeding a finch, learns quickly that it is constantly teaching him. The best placement of a litter box, letting the horse see your approach, and placing the millet branch on the side of the cage are all examples of functional etiquette the owner learns with help from the animal. For millennia, humans have not only been in close contact with wild animals but have trained them to answer human needs whether they be utilitarian or artistic. Again, the animals let the humans know what they prefer even in captivity. Some even let the humans believe the illusion that they, the humans, are ultimately in charge. When that is out of a person's focus, disaster strikes. Everyone knows stories about trainers who have faced severe tragedy when forgetting that even trained wild animals are wild.

Perhaps the most domesticated of wild species is the Asian elephant. These large mammals have been taking orders in all languages and complying whether it be in the Southeastern Asian lumber industry, agriculture, or the center ring of a circus. But confuse them about what is around the area of their feet, which they cannot see, and they resort to hostile stomping and offensive headstands on the culprit. Most sadly, this happens when a female gives birth for the first time after twenty-two months of gestation. She doesn't know what is happening to her, and suddenly something is messing with her hind feet. Breeders learn fast to remove the newborn instantly before it is trampled. Dangerous wild animals have long taught humans their interpretations of danger.

There is a well-known story told about the great gorilla Gargantua, the prized ape exhibited for years by the Ringling Brothers and Barnum and Bailey

Circus after a childhood spent as "Buddy" in a private home. Handlers and caregivers found out early on that Gargantua would avoid aggression if an ordinary flashlight were focused on his eyes. That enabled safe entry to service his cage. Another trick played on the first great ape so many Americans ever saw was based on his love for a bottle of Coke. He would be teased with the bottle until he was just about in a rage, and when the bottle was finally given to him, he would gulp it down manically only to find out it was his regular dose of cascara!

Why bother the wild animals anyway? Cannot they simply be left alone for their own peace and well-being, as well as ours? Apart from inevitable meet-ups on a shrinking planet, of course they can. Whether they should be left alone opens a rich ethical speculation as old as the story of Genesis. Apart from the DNA we almost completely share with certain species, we also share enough consciousness to register each other's consciousness. Eye contact with any animal brings this home dramatically, and such connecting prompts speech—and not just from humans. If there is any suggestion of an animal reply, via movement, grunt, whine, chirp, or even roar, some measure of romance may be on its way.

The truth is, we are animals, and as such, we share the animal kingdom. Self-conscious sharing of that

kingdom can educate us about the dynamics of relationship, and because such sharing is cross-*species*, there
is the undoubtable development of cross-*class* sensitivi-
ties with fellow humans. The occasional complaint "I
just wish she'd show some of the affection she lavishes
on that dog to her son" says it all. By obvious exten-
sion, any increased social behavior skills are worth developing, especially in so-called iphone societies with
their isolated individuals. The increasing use of care animals in various health situations seems a poignant development. Whether the myriad animal rights groups
approve or not, animals have a beneficent effect on human beings. Given proper care of the animals, how can
that be bad?

The effect of human beings on wild animals is, of
course, more complicated, but there is evidence that
good comes from acknowledging that animals have a
"right to work." In the 1990s, a large circus with fifteen Asian elephants and one African elephant allowed
a university veterinary college to monitor the behavior
of all sixteen elephants twenty-four-seven for a month.
The surveillance was intended to reveal symptoms of
stress. The results were not altogether surprising. The
fifteen animals who worked in tent setup and performance did not show signs of stress, whereas the African
elephant, carried for educational exhibition only, did
register stress.

Anyone visiting a zoo with a successful bonobo breeding program can notice the difference in the animals after their midday enrichment session with handlers. They are much livelier and inventive in their play and teasing of each other. The so-called "environment enrichment" programs are largely successful in breaking monotony and "teasing" problem-solving and other creativity from the animals.

Zoos can be learning opportunities for the generation that needs to grow in their understanding of the food chain. More than my own romantic fascination can begin through the glass or caging of the ape collection. How often a reserved, beautifully groomed, attractive young lady falls in fascination with an unkempt "old man of the forest" while watching the orangutans. Eye movements and unreserved eye contact are so compelling, as are the even delicate movements of gigantic hands and fingers. Such are happy moments, indeed. But then the chance glimpse of a colorful data-posting injects fear and sadness into the rich relationship. "How are they doing?" Perhaps every exhibit in the zoological collection has such a posting. It refers to the species or subspecies population remaining in the wild. Alas, the orangutans are among the most endangered of all species. They exist only in Borneo and Sumatra, host countries to expansive and always-expanding palm oil plantations that directly and seriously impinge on the habitat of our orangutan friends. The forest of the "old man of the forest" is vanishing, and with it, the magnificent creatures who owned it first.

Given the noticeable rise in controversy over exhibited and performing animals, it is hard to disclose objectivity about what the animals actually experience. "Are they happy?" seems a reasonable-enough question, but uncovering an answer is extremely difficult given myriad biases in the matter. "They're not *meant* to do that" and similar attitudes get most of the mileage until questions like "Who's doing the *meaning?*" and the examples of child performers flying through the air are adduced. If it's possible and safe, why shouldn't an animal be applauded for balancing on a ball and rolling it across a plank as the band plays celebratory music? Observation of performance animals as their time to be displayed approaches can be indicative. So often, there is not only readiness but an eager approach to the ring and an automatic launch into the learned behaviors. It should be noted that the use of force or threat is not at all as present as the use of positive reinforcement or rewards for successful accomplishments. How often performing animals who have missed a trick bounce front and center to try again.

*Author's horses teaching him what a
circus liberty act is all about.*

A performing horse, retired after years of entertaining the public, was brought to the ring to demonstrate how much he remembered. Not only did he execute his behaviors in their consecrated order, but he remembered a behavior the trainer had forgotten, nudged the trainer out of the way, and went on with the routine. There are even cases of animals escaping only to enter the big top and make their way to the ring. Typically, they are finally apprehended only after completing their act, though almost no one else is in the tent.

Much of the time, affection for animals seems to trump frigid respect for them. Is the affection returned?

Every night after the shows, a lone circus clown walked past a caged rhinoceros display on his way back to his trailer. The rhino was carried only as an educational aspect of the menagerie. The repeated experience of fascinated crowds who had never seen such an animal seemed to warrant such an exhibit. But at night, when the audiences were gone and most of the show was packed up, ready for an early morning departure, the clown would stand at one end of the rhino's enclosure. The great, two-ton pachyderm would lumber down to the bars and wait for a—yes, loving—goodnight pat on the cheek. Affection both ways?

One night, after the clown and most of the circus had fallen asleep, he was awakened by the sound of rustling outside his trailer window. It sounded distinctly like an elephant shaking out bags of garbage behind the concession trailer. A groggy check through the window revealed that exact scene. So, the clown dressed, snuck out of his trailer, and went over to that of the elephant department boss.

A light knock summoned a sleepy "Yeah?"

"You'd better get up, Johnny. One of your girls is over behind the concession trailer."

"Okay, I'll be right there."

Minutes later, a touching drama unfolded that few people ever get to enjoy.

The "boss" just watched and smiled, and then he

quietly asked, "Barbara, what are you doing?"

A calm turn of the large head revealed all the guilt of a little kid caught in the cookie jar.

"Now, go back home."

And Barbara turned all of her tonnage in the direction she'd come while Johnny and the clown watched. Without any further communication, she found her way back to her truck and waited to be secured. In this case, a pile of bags containing sticky remains of cotton candy substituted for the cookie jar. But there didn't seem to be any fear in the air anywhere, just lots of "I can't let him down."

Sweet tastes are only one positive fascination for Asian elephants. Barbara's companion Susie, in the same herd, was all saddled up one evening before a performance. She loved to give rides, but as her handler was speaking with a clown friend, the clown suddenly felt a nudge to his stomach. Looking down, he beheld the end of Susie's trunk making its way up his chest and then to his ruff collar. She was checking out the scent the clown had spritzed his collar with. No one knew she was a Polo fan.

At the end, of course, we can only guess what really motivates wild animals and where and when there could be emotion. We can only read the signs of affection that we assess as such in the behaviors of domestic animals. Even with cats and dogs, there is a lot of surmise in our too-often anthropomorphizing about Felix and Fido. Sadly, we only half admit the silliness of "She knows I'm going to the store" or "He just loves to watch *America's Got Talent*."

The obvious bottom line is that we share the earth with the other animals. As early as the oral tradition that got recorded in the sixth to fifth centuries BCE, the conviction that animals were here first was noted. Anyone convinced of the science behind the sea being the beginning of evolutionary life will note that the creation of the sea predates Eden. So what? To what have we now evolved?

Presently, we are left to responsibly cohabit a shrinking globe. Once, a very small circus that traveled in one van was making its way across Chicago on a busy street when there was a commotion at the passengers' feet. Tired of her dull surroundings in a cage parked at the van's rear end, a mature spider monkey had freed herself and was confidently marching up to the cab, where she climbed onto the dashboard and took in the view. "Back there" had become "here." "They" had become "we." Respect must be a common denominator, and admiration for *other* must be a welcome emotion. Injury and fear must surrender to respect and kindness. Thrift must increasingly counter expense, conservancy must reform mindless usage, and open arms must replace crossed ones.

Wherever evolution is headed, it will be infused with the effects of human intelligence. And if the mind can mean anything, it is above all the agent of unity in our lives and those of our fellows. It has to form relationships, unities. Fragmentation seems an agent of resistance to the direction everything has been headed. Is fusion better than fission? Is something good just because it has been invented?

Or is the existential capacity for unity, from the atomic level to the social, what gives ultimate shape and dynamism to whatever we are readying for the next level of being?

Oh, there's the bell. Fun's over. Let's see. "Well, how was recess?" might be the first question in class. Might the answer be another question? "Is the existential capacity for unity, from the atomic level to the social, what gives ultimate shape and dynamism to whatever we are readying for the next level of being?"

Fun, huh?

13

VOICES AND GLIMPSES

AND SO IT goes, the seldom-ending whirl of voices remembered and present that usually provoke serious thought even when not intending to. The large, multi-block quadrangle of a morning walk joins the carousel of remembered statements and incidents in providing an ample library of reflections. That walk might just include the first bird calls of the day as multiple species look for their counterparts; a dozen walked dogs sniffing for a public place to accommodate private business; up to seven different bus stops for three different routes; a grocery store; a river, a church, and a school; a well- taverned bohemian section; a very unpretentious coffee shop, a drugstore, and half a dozen panhandlers. Any one, and sometimes several, of these stimulants can recall, rebut, or reinforce snippets of remembered statements emerging from the memory's whirlwind.

So often, wherever casual converse brushes up against anything like philosophy, the tautology of "It is what it is" finds voice. Most often, this follows an expression of something unpleasant that must be accepted or dealt with in life. Probably both speaker and hearer accept such a statement as a realistic solution, or at least a palliative. Secretly both parties must sense that it is no such thing. Not only is that nonsensical statement true, but its correlative, "It is what it *isn't*" is equally true because the unpleasant side of the situation is what likely perdures, not an imaginable situation that presently doesn't exist or for now *isn't*. This nagging notion, that what isn't more convenient actually exists, is the overture to a litany of questions all bearing on what it would take to make things better: *what if, what would it take, would it be better, might there be, could it happen that...* By admitting the negative correlative, the possibility of a solution comes into view.

Any discussion of *truth* must eventually admit that it occurs in a frigid context of the *false*. One highlights the other. No matter how earnestly one seeks truth, one begins and continues that pursuit to avoid the false. To be fair, "It is what it is" is profoundly philosophical, even Greek. The truth *is*. What enjoys being, or existence, is true. To remark that something does not exist is also to remark a truth. Hence, the seeming tautology "It is what it is" mightily suggests what isn't, and that suggestion is also the truth.

So, which is true? Both. But don't bring this stuff up at recess.

We seem to endlessly collect data or evidence, true or false, and it is an often unconscious drive to determine that which drives us most profoundly, the pursuit of truth. It seems even healthy to align one's talents with such a drive. There is at least a nagging suspicion that we are meant for truth and indulging such a vital purpose feeds us in life-building dimensions. Truth and health seem to be in cahoots.

After recess, the older kids might encounter a Latin teacher's nearly flippant "mens sana in corpore sano." No one, not even the teacher, need know that the words are stolen from the Latin poet Juvenal. Even in the late first century CE, folks were stealing ideas from the ancient Greeks about the relationship between mind and body. And today, the impulse toward such thinking may be the energy in our intense pursuit of the mechanical side of the brain and nervous system: the stimulus-response network perceiving *what is* and the very real implication of *what isn't*.

It seems that daily the quest increases for the infinitesimal lightning enabling our consciousness to be rooted and routed through a very material nervous network. Gone and going are the spookier presumptions that thought and the psyche are spiritual. And if synaptic electricity can be observed, detected, and affected? What we do with its stuff and the stuff surrounding it—all that *corpus sanum*—will either improve or hinder the output of that very material *mens*.

In fact, Juvenal conceived the *mens* to be quite independent of the *corpus*. He seems only concerned that both components, the mind and the body, be well. Neither he nor his fellow philosophers considered the two to be a physical entity. The health of both, though, seemed somehow paramount if the compound that is a human was to be in health.

Today we see a physician about matters of bodily well-being. We believe he is a *heal*-er maintaining our *heal*th. When serious mood shifts suggest something not-so-organic might be awry, he invokes the specialty of the psychiatrist, another healer who treats the body to some very material medicines that affect outlook, mood, and even very material productivity. Most often, the psychiatrist will work with a psychologist whose "talk therapy" approach quite often uncovers more of the "who" a person is than the "what" a person can be. But even here, the physicality of the person's life is constantly addressed: What do you *do*? *What* happened? *Whom* do you miss? *How much* do you exercise?

All of this contributes to our conviction that if you stay physically healthy, you will be mentally healthy. The organic unity seems even more enforced when the proposition is reversed: if you maintain a healthy attitude toward your body's well-being, it will be a more dependable support for your whole person. The emphasis, thus, has become one of mind-body unity as a given person seeks success in life.

Of course, success in life is an unwieldy concept because it assumes so many postures and is assessed with such an array of very different criteria. "She could be a very successful mortician" really opens the mind to a far different future than does "He is meant to be a construction engineer."

The word *success* is itself unwieldy. Etymologically it seems too identified with the Latin and the politics behind *succession*: *succedere,* meaning to follow close behind, makes all kinds of sense in the history of royal politics and much less sense in attributing masterful achievement in a human endeavor regardless of rank. Sadly, it is too often identified with social status and specifically a level of income.

In a more accessible, perhaps truthful sense, *success* might be seen as a twofold achievement in one professional pursuit. Granted the state of accomplishment and skill that is mastery, the word also connotes a state of well-being in the master. The mortician has mastered the skills of life, say, raising her family, as well as a scientific and sensitive caring for the deceased who are carried to her. The engineer can effectively read blueprints for a skyscraper and help his buddies understand new benefits and possible shortcomings in a union proposal. There could be more. Whether cause or effect, success is always a very close neighbor of happiness in a human personality. The man or woman is complete in a certain content with the way his or her life transpires. Without surrendering to laziness at all, there is an acceptance of the situation right alongside constant striving for better performance in every aspect of one's life. An enduring atmosphere is enjoyed in which such striving, such work, hardly seems like work at all.

What is work? Minimally, it is directed effort. Something is perceived as a needed change in the way things are. This blank screen, occurring at this point in my manuscript needs words shedding some kind of light on what work is. Usually, in a discussion of work, it is the effort involved that receives the most attention. How difficult, technical, unusual, demanding the effort required becomes almost synonymous with work. In the present project, the actual physicality of the effort, the typing, requires no recognizable effort at all. The mental effort to find correct or accurate words is another matter. It is the imagination in such an effort that so often makes beginning a writing session difficult. In that sense, the process becomes work. Blessedly, the process sustains itself once a beginning is made and the journey through a topic is begun.

May a given work project be seen as effecting needed change? Here the concept of work takes on a social tone. Change seems beyond the effort of a given project. It could involve more than just the state of the worker. And since the need for change has already been determined, it just might be beyond the control and ken of the one doing the work. In the present example, the written development of this topic has already been called for in preparatory outline. Such preparation follows the decision to write the entire manuscript, which, it is deemed, may benefit—at least modestly change— a reader or two. In the course of realizing this written project, the writer's own thought processes about the subject of work itself become clearer, fuller, richer, perhaps even making the next step in this effort somewhat easier.

Work itself, rightly understood and undertaken, changes the worker as it satisfies the need for a social change. In the present case, it changes how work is perceived and then undertaken in the future. Objective and subjective change occurs simultaneously.

The quality of that change is another matter. A comparison between the present writing achievement and this morning's encounter with a supermarket checkout employee could be illuminating. A committee meeting has long ago decided that with the advent of scanning technology, checking out thousands of grocery items an hour should become almost mindless for a given clerk and her bagger. Enter a slightly distracted writer with a few items of produce to purchase. Long before this entrance, clerk and bagger have opened up a quite warm replay of last night's encounters with friends. The writer's "Good morning" is not heard or is ignored in deference to the latest detail in so-and-so's romance. The scanner's bell seems to be trying to interrupt the low-volume, high-interest conversation but cannot. The items pass to the bagger, and the computer printer pushes up the receipt, which seems to have a voice: "Have a good day."

Said clerk came to "work" this morning and,

indeed, was seen scanning for hours. Such scanning really had long ago changed the environment and experience of grocery shopping. Sadly, it had nothing to do with changing the clerk short of tiring her. The only modification possible had to occur inside the exchange of stories with the bagger. The writer and his produce, money, and greeting did not effectively exist. So much for social change through work.

On the other hand, the writer went down to the office of the service coordinator where he lives. Long ago, someone or a committee determined that such an office in a HUD facility of fourteen floors would effect meaningful change and improved quality in tenants' lives. Today the writer needed a cane, and the coordinator interrupted her office work to accommodate by visiting a storage locker on the property, finding a cane, and giving it to him. While the effort involved was minimal, it was focused and improved both parties: allowing the coordinator an added insight to the writer's increasing sense of instability and giving the writer assurance of his balance so that he could pursue his walking exercise.

Then there is the "fit" of a job, as in the expression "She was made for that job; it really fits her." Somehow, the execution of a job's requirements seems easy for such an individual; so little effort is evident in fulfilling them. Besides, the efforts that are expended produce splendid results, often beyond expectations.

Personally, such individuals are not aware of their efforts. The work is so compatible with their personalities that it seems to actually complement who they are. They are comfortable just doing what they do. "It's what I do" expresses what is experienced as effortless, no matter the success of the project. And success is so common that there is a personal satisfaction in actual job performance; the "laborer" experiences what can only be called deep joy in her profession. Indeed, "It hardly seems like work at all."

Sadly, that experience of personal joy is too seldom expressed. It's as though it is not understood in human experience and therefore not discussed. Many seem artificial—"phony"—to themselves when describing their feelings as joyful. Such a word is "over the top" and therefore inappropriate for day-to-day converse.

What an emotional shortchange such holding back is. Because we don't fully understand our experience of joy, we won't admit it. We experience it all the time; however, we won't talk about it. "I am a joyful person" seems so much more dishonest than "I'm a hardworking person," "I'm an independent person," or "I'm by nature pretty negative." Just the word *joy* feels stretched.

Yet we laugh and play all the time. What is going on internally that produces those actions? Mistaken or not, a good laugh connotes a balance of insights and self-acceptance that sets us on an almost uncontrolled reflex, whether chuckle or roar.

How sad are such expressions as "joy juice" or "joy-ride," referring to deliberate and mechanical efforts to produce interior sensations that are careless and care-free. In such experiences, the self is almost obliterated from whatever entertainment it brings on itself, whereas the intense sensation of integrity in one's work, of identity and expanse in appreciation of art, or of human contradictions in comedy always confronts a very present self. In fact, it is hard to imagine joy disembodied from the human encounter with it. Joy seems only able to exist in the human experience of it.

It could be that the self must have a capacity for joyfulness to perceive it and experience it. Could it be self-intensifying, so that the more I laugh and smile and affirm the presence of happiness, the more joyful I am and the more capable of experiencing the joyful qualities of my daily adventures? Joy seems to feed itself if given a chance.

Maybe too much is expected of joy because it is so commonly appropriated by religious expression. In this way, joy seems only possible with a visit from "on high" or in so-called *sacred* occasions. And since religious encounters are understood to be rare and rarified, the usage of *joy* as describing a human reaction or disposition is rare. But the emotions stirred as joyful are profoundly human and not rarified at all. So, the perception of incongruity in a good dirty joke can trigger as genuine a joyful response as a kiss among the lilies at a high church wedding. One doesn't need organ music to be joyful; one needs the acceptance of self as part of the happy wonder that is existence itself—even in the little parts of it we get to experience.

Whew! Did that sound philosophical? What's wrong with philosophy? It's just the complex of efforts we make to figure out what the *is* is in *what it is*. And if that includes the existence of joy, why not enjoy it? Even in Metaphysics Class 101.

Usually, a healthy notion of joy understands it as a disposition, a characteristic, an atmosphere in which an individual traverses the adventures of his life. It's just about a virtue if you read Paul or whoever wrote the letter to the Galatians. There it becomes a "fruit" of the gifts of the Spirit, something enjoyed because of a gift. And in such a context, it just about seems like something the individual is commissioned to work at, to develop, to—well, uh, *enjoy*. In that context, it is far from an attribute to be ashamed of or hidden.

Whatever joy is, however it is understood, it is expansive. It makes one feel richer, fuller. It also seems contagious. One of its characteristics, laughter, is readily admitted to being socially exchanged, much like a contagion. It's usually hard not to laugh with sincere laughers (even sitting in the dark at the theater or cinema). Perhaps for this reason, they seem to find a ready social welcome wherever they go. They seem to be a gift to their varied communities. Their readiness to express happiness seems to call up a similar disposition from their companions so that their gift becomes valued.

Gifts seem to have different levels and requirements for value. Of course, their intrinsic value may have readily identifiable worth. But their interplay with the history of a relationship between the giver and receiver also connotes value at perhaps the most significant level. That there occurs the actual giving of the gift proclaims or celebrates the giver-receiver relationship itself.

Whatever the nature of the gift, it seems to be a symbol or representation of the self of the giver. "I value you significantly, and I want you to know it; therefore, please accept this token of myself." And so often the gift itself represents some aspect of the giver-receiver relationship's history: something echoing a commonly shared moment in time.

The person receiving such a gift must recognize something of herself in the gift: a favorite color, flower, fabric, photo, or event. But just as important is the gift's reflection of the giver. The object itself must be reflective of the giver. At first, this seems contradictory, but what else can make the presentation of the gift personally unique?

Say two close friends make a trip to Yosemite National Park. Filled with adventure and splendid vistas of nature, there is yet a detail that one friend cherishes more than any other: a humble pinecone two squirrels are wrestling with outside the friends' tent. Unbeknownst to the enchanted friend, that memorial of the trip makes it back to the Midwestern city the two call home. There it is: a friend bespeaks his care for a vacation companion by preserving something the companion values. But there is a seeming increase in the exchange's power if the scenario is reversed in a way. Obviously, they both enjoyed the pinecone-squirrel tussle. What if the most affected companion secretly transports the cone home and gives it to the other companion? The receiver recognizes how much he is cared for since the gift has meant so much to the giver. An amazing chemistry.

Of course, the value of the gift resonates with the intensity of the relationship. Aside from anything like monetary worth, such value reflects how much a friendship means to both friends. So much of a friendship can be taken for granted so that when a gift "happens" on the scene, there is a focus on just what the friendship means. But this focus is not only had by the giver; the receiver is compelled to stop, look, and listen to just what she has in this companionship. Consequently, the presentation of the gift intensifies the relationship. And this can all be possible with just the unexpected presentation of a single gift. In fact, the focus in such an event nearly outshines that of a customary exchange of gifts, say, at Christmas or an anniversary celebration. When gifts are expected to be part of the atmosphere, they can lose their intensity as compared to gifts given spontaneously and unexpectedly. And in the unexpected, non-prescribed presentation of an object very closely tied with the identity of the giver, there is just about a proclamation of how much the giver values the relationship. "Here is something of me" seems to hang in the air.

Of course, any discussion of the intensity of personal relationships eventually introduces the issue of types or levels of relationships, of which there just might be as many as there are friendships. The very unicity inherent in the notion of person dictates that any and every combination of personalities must be unique, hence the strong emotional undercurrent charging the presentation of the simplest gift: this stands for me and also for our relationship, which I treasure. In such a context, the commonest shelf item might become a jewel.

So often, the warmth of interpersonal relationships is just about refrigerated in sloppy sociological typology of friendships. "Oh, he's just a friend!" says so much and so little at the same time. A distinction is obviously intended, but what is said about the speaker's attitude toward friendship in general and this one in particular? "He's not special enough to be my lover" hovers in the background of such an announcement. But too often, another shortchange is implied: that the love in question is *just* a caliber of whatever friendship is. Absent is any notion that what the speaker enjoys with her friend is just as special and humanly intense as what she enjoys with her lover. That there is a completely different quality in the two loves and not just a different intensity seems ignored or irrelevant. Yet discussions of marital quality can so often hinge on the issue of friendship.

Perhaps as important as the bonding always underlying any kind of relationship between friends is the atmosphere of freedom in which such a relationship thrives. No one has to have anyone else as a friend. Staggering. What would human life be without friendship? And is it possible that humanity could not exist?

Imagine ten people: a high school graduate seeing her gift of a brand new car; a zookeeper hand-feeding a baby camel; a friend having just heard of another friend's failed, long-time romance; two newlyweds; a five-year-old spying a bin of banana chips in the grocery store; Julia Child demonstrating a new casserole recipe; a Cistercian monk deep in prayer; a casual friend and neighbor who has just noticed his neighbor's care for another friend; and an early-morning writer seeing his favorite photo of a child posted as his laptop's wallpaper.

That's right! They all have something in common. But it's not an emotion. It's what they say about an emotion they think they're experiencing and that may very well be different in each case. They all use the expression "I love" in the given situation.

The high school grad circling the new car says to her parents, "I love it!"; the zookeeper coos her "I love you!" as she offers the bottle to the camel; The friend might take the other friend's hand sometime during the story of the romantic failure and, at the end, say, "I love you"; the newlyweds are hard-pressed to find new ways of saying an obvious "I love you"; the five-year-old in the grocery story yells out, "Oh, I love these," as she sneaks her hand into the bin of chips; Julia's falsetto registers utter salivation as she shakes the paprika can and sings, "I just love the way the paprika zings out the cucumber's very own taste"; the monk may be lost in a meditation that only ends in "I love you"; the casual friend tosses off an "I love that guy!" that surprises him and the friends who hear him; and the writer has to hold back from touching the little kid's nose in the photo as he says his usual "Why do I love a little knucklehead?"

While it may not be clear what a given speaker means in his or her situation, it is clear that they all use some variation of the expression "I love you" to reflect a varying emotion, feeling, or impulse, and it is also quite certain that each of these folks is having a different experience of what they're calling *love*.

The graduate instantly imagines herself driving the vehicle and what it will say about her; it may be tantamount to a new outfit. The zookeeper, with perhaps a protective warmth toward the awkward steps of a newborn, is admiring the beauty inherent in an exact miniature of the camel's mother. Hearing of the friend's failure in romance, the other friend has sensed the resultant weakness and literally "reaches out" with an "I love you" that says merely, "I'm here for you to talk to anytime." Such a love suggests it may be easier to be without a lover than to be without this kind of friend. The five-year-old is simply remembering how good banana chips taste in her mouth. Julia likes cucumbers. Depending on how his imagination reacts to his mode of contact with an ultimate source, the monk may actually be united in love with another. The casual friend has just experienced a moment of humanity in someone he doesn't know very well, and he expresses himself dramatically. As for the writer, it could be he imagines the child in the photo to be as fascinated with him as he is with the child's beauty. What he says to the kid is possibly an effort to get a toddler's giggle out of himself.

Oh, those two lovers? One is saying what he knows the other is thinking, and they are both compelled in their conviction that they are each having the same experience. In this case, "I love you" stumbles to be the expression of the "real deal."

The chief hurdle in any detailed discussion of human love is our minuscule understanding of the brain's operation in such an intense experience. Approaching that experience from the details of oral expression is very likely to be superficial since speech can so rarely match the brain in what passes for comprehension. Thus, the reaction to the new car is a vocal flare-up, a reaction to the flash of chrome and color before there is time to realize the why of it all and the teary-eyed vocalization of what it's really all about: the love of the parents. Then the words will change to "I love you" in the gratitude of an intense embrace.

But even experiential descriptions of the so-called "real deal" can seem superficial, and the happy result of such a failure may be the successful art that emerges, say, poetry or song. Truth be told, for all the "when it happens, you'll know" about the subject, we don't know very much or can't say very much about exactly what love is. It is intense, sometimes suddenly consuming, pleasant enough to be almost always welcome. But what is it? Sex is related to it but is an intensely physical and largely temporary expression of love; friendship seems somewhere on a continuum with the energy we call love, but without the emotional intensity. There is a distinct difference between "She is my friend" and "She is my lover." In such a distinction, the difference seems one of intensity and completeness, and it seems easier to be without a friend that it is to be without a lover.

But what constitutes that intensity and completeness?

Experientially considered, there is something of a mirror in every expression of love. In what is loved, there is a heavy intimation of self. The car, the baby camel, the romantic friend, the banana chips and cucumbers, certainly the newlywed, and the laptop's wallpaper all resonate with the self at a level more or less intense. And that resonance is personal: the very subjective object speaks to the lover as if it were a talking mirror. Possession, acquaintance, taste, intensity, romance, and friendship all reflect and potentially enlarge the lover's or "lover's" self-concept. Seen from such a perspective, love seems necessarily, automatically, and constructively selfish.

In an important sense, love has to be selfish, if not self-centered. Prescinding cucumbers, cars, chips, and camels, couples in love notoriously gaze into each other's eyes. Those facial features have fairly or unfairly been dubbed the windows of the soul because everyone recognizes that the eye is a present and exact recording of what it is looking at. And if one pair of eyes is recording the recording of another pair of eyes, a rather intense exchange occurs. Often it is too intense, as with mere or occasional friends, and one or both sets of eyes break or lose contact. "Look me in the eye" is not only a command; it is a command to be tested. Translated, it might become "Can you look me in the eye?" But between lovers, eyes have been dubbed the windows of the soul because of the seeming psychic nakedness free and mutual gazing produces. "I have nothing to hide from you, nor do I want to hide anything.

Staying with the situation of serious lovers, the self-centeredness of offered love seems critical. One lover, recognizing the love returned, is assured that she is loveable and, in turn, returns more in a self-intensifying exchange that endlessly bonds. In its purest form, love must be a self who assures another assuring self. As a caveat, *selfishness* can derail the mutuality in that it steals from what is offered. And as a bonus, genuine *self-love, -care,-improvement* increase the capacity of self's gift.

Lest such a description seem a limiting or mutually selfish rendering of love, the development of self must not be imagined apart from the world and society. A lover finds his love as she is interacting with what she knows of her society. That complex of skills is part of her gift to him, and vice versa. It should stand to reason that self-improvement embraces more of the world with the unique talents that any given personality has. More, a bonded relationship of such talents could be seen as an original contribution to society. Where there is love, there is more: more of humanity, more of potential.

The strength and applicability of love's bonding calls for examination. Might all successful growth in existence originate in the drive toward unification or bonding? Are the principles of general relativity and special relativity possible precisely because of a universal "yearning" for what is seemingly apart to be seen as "related"? For that matter, is not science itself possible because nature is connected—bonded, in so many ways? On his way to developing the theory of special relativity, Einstein became distressed that the electromagnetic evidence before him could not be explained with Newtonian mechanics and the resulting dualism was insupportable. What does math's mighty equal sign mean if not relation and some degree of bonding? Density, gravity, coherence—even at the atomic and subatomic level—all bespeak the electric drive to unity that climbs through the molecular, cellular, and material world. Is that world actually in love with itself? And if love is potential, if it is indeed more, could not a planet's self-love not explain the expansion of the universe that so troubled Einstein toward the end of his quest? In this light, our so-human genius himself becomes a symbol of the universe: intensely loving the love story of earth, he became a troubled witness to the ever-increasing love throughout existence.

From so many perspectives, love really is all, and it connects even the humblest of lovers with the most important forces possible, forces not yet imagined even in the mightiest of recess times.

BIBLIOGRAPHY

Cain, Bill: *Equivocation; 9 Circles; How to Write a New Book for the Bible*

Chardin, Teilhard: *The Divine Milieu*

Desmond, Matthew: *Evicted: Poverty and Profit in the American City*

Harari, Yuval Noah: *Sapiens: A Brief History of Humankind; Homo Deus: A Brief History of Tomorrow; 21 Lessons for the 21st Century*

Isaacson, Walter: *Einstein: His Life and Universe*

Kuhn, Joaqin and Feeney, Joseph J.: *Hopkins Variations: Standing round a Waterfall*

Lonergan, Bernard J.F.: *Insight: A Study of Human Understanding*

Mackenzie, Norman H.: *A Reader's Guide to Gerard Manley Hopkins*

Nutt, Amy Ellis: *Becoming Nicole: The Transformation of an American Family*

Pollan, Michael: *The Omnivore's Dilemma*

Sartre, Jean Paul: *No Exit*

Shakespeare, William: *Romeo and Juliet; Othello; The Tempest; Henry IV, Part One; Macbeth; Hamlet;* "Sonnet 29"

Acknowledgements

Many thanks to Bill Cain, SJ, Kevin Curdt, Barbara Mickelson, Judie Gillespie and Carlo Pellegrini for their early readings of the text and their encouragement. Appreciation also goes out to Jenny Pratt and Julie Owen for their example, understanding and kindness. The writer is indebted to Jefferson at First Edit for very helpful line editing and sentence adjustments. The author's online presence is made possible by the generosity of Jean Moreland. Artistic example and support came abundantly from Kylle St. Trail.